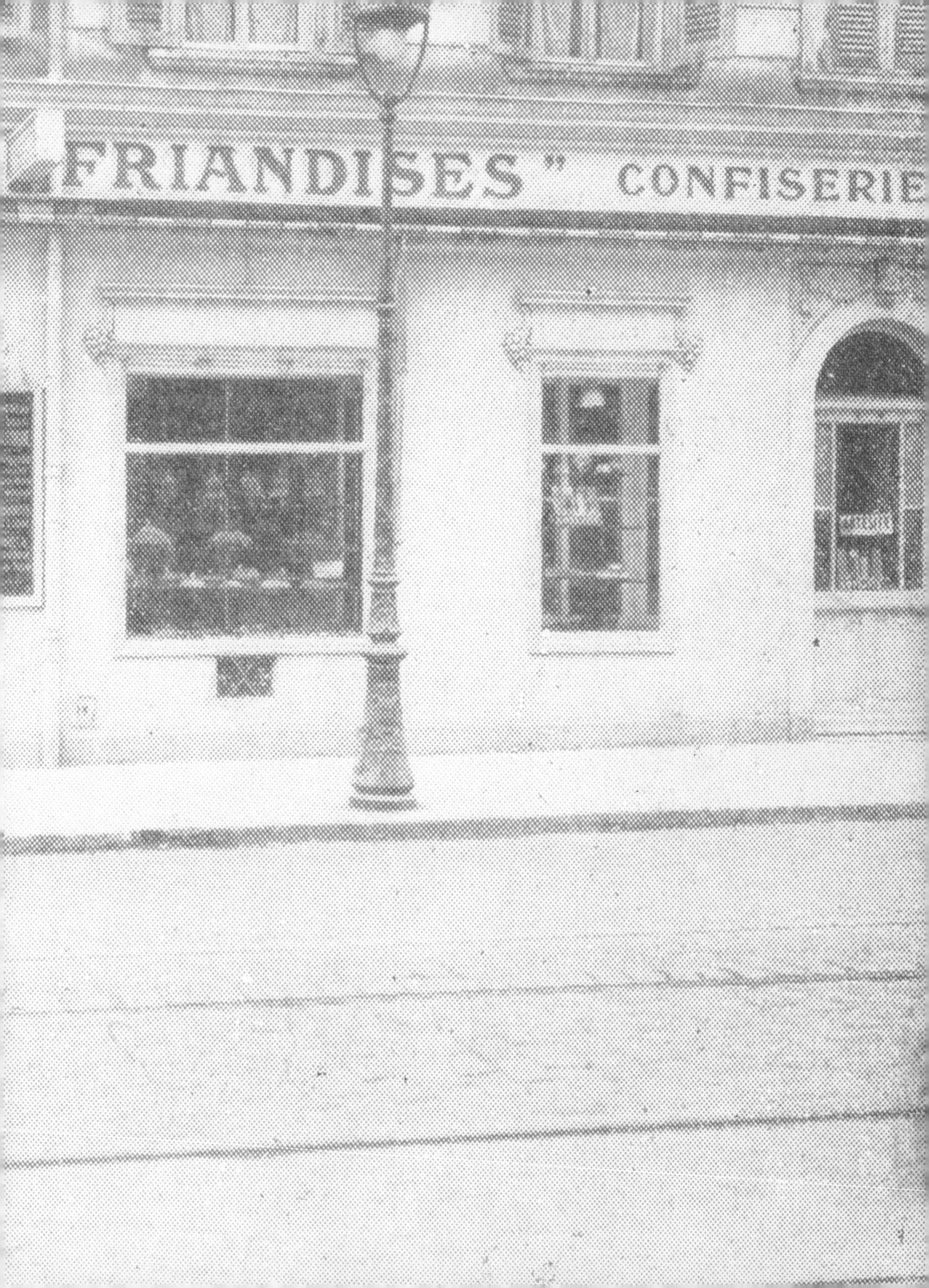
FRIANDISES "
CONFISERIE

Simply
Sensational
Desserts

Photographs by Philippe Houze

Broadway Books
New York

Simply Sensational Desserts

140 Classics for

the Home Baker

from New York's

Famous Pâtisserie

and Bistro

François Payard

with Tim Moriarty and Tish Boyle

Library of Congress Cataloging-in-Publication Data
Payard, François.
Simply sensational desserts : 140 classics for the home baker from
New York's famous pâtisserie and bistro / François Payard,
with Tim Moriarty and Tish Boyle. — 1st ed.
p.   cm.
Includes index.
ISBN 0-7679-0358-7 (hc.)
1. Desserts.   I. Moriarty, Tim.   II. Boyle, Tish.   III. Title.
TX773.P36   1999
641.8'6—DC21   99-19204
CIP

FIRST EDITION

Designed by Ralph L. Fowler

00   01   02   03   10 9 8 7 6 5 4 3

To my grandfather

Charles Henry,

whose artistry and passion for pastry

inspired both my father and myself.

Contents

Preface

FRIENDSHIP AND DEEP RESPECT are just a part of what François Payard and I share. We also have in common a passion for the cuisine of Provence, crystallized through our mutual heritage of the flavors of the French Riviera. It is that combination of sweetness and bitterness, subtlety and vigor, that delights the senses beneath the omnipresent, golden Mediterranean sun.

We claim this inheritance from our fathers, who are talented chefs and great teachers, as well as from the many prestigious chefs who have preceded us over the centuries. These are the people who laid the foundation for, and continue to inspire, the cuisine that we produce each day.

The creation of great desserts is an art, and François Payard excels at that art. That he chose to offer his talent on the other side of the Atlantic is a delight to some and a regret to those left behind. Above all, it is an adventure.

This book is a testament to François's generosity and his willingness to share what he has learned. The true strength of this book lies in this: François's magic with desserts is now accessible to anyone willing to learn. The nuances of flavor and secrets of technique found in these pages will be a treasure for the lover of "Grand Cuisine"—and to anyone who enjoys a great dessert.

Alain Ducasse

Acknowledgments

SPECIAL THANKS TO Alexandra, who helped me prepare this book and who is always there to push me to greater heights and support me when I arrive. To Tish Boyle and Tim Moriarty for their great efforts; they never got discouraged. To Jonathan Ducrest, my personal assistant, who is so dedicated to helping me run my establishment and who is so professional, so young! Thanks also for the support from all of my friends and collaborators in the field, especially Hervé Poussot, Florian Bellanger of Le Bernardin, and Nicolas Berger.

I must also thank all of the people who have worked with me and for me, especially Nancy Keshner, Johnny Izzuni, Gregory Goureau, David Carmichael, and Lincoln Carson. And to the people who have helped me to become a pastry chef and restaurateur: Monsieur and Madame Senderens, the late Gilbert LeCoze and Maguy LeCoze, Eric Ripert, my partner Daniel Boulud and his wife, Mickey (for her help and good ideas), and my investor, Joel Smilow. And to both Georgette Farkas and my controller, Marcel Doron, for helping to open Payard Pâtisserie and Bistro.

Thanks also to Keli Bates for her efforts in testing the recipes—especially after a twelve-hour shift. To John from Riviera Products for bringing the best ingredients and fruits for the preparation of the recipes. To Brian Maynard, from KitchenAid, for his generosity in providing equipment. To Bernardaud and Dominique Millet for their generous loan of the china and accessories seen in the photos. To my good friend and executive chef Philippe Bertineau for exchanging ideas and invaluable help in preparing this book. To Harriet Bell for her support and outstanding collaboration. To my agent, Bob Tabian, for his understanding and tireless fight to find the best editor for *Simply Sensational Desserts*. To Alexis Levenson at Broadway Books for her patience and help. To Philippe Houze for the great photographs in this book. To Alain Ducasse for taking the time from his busy schedule to write the generous words in the preface. To my family as well as my wife Alexandra's parents for their support and help. Thanks to all the staff at Payard Pâtisserie and Bistro for supporting me during the craziness of the holidays and the ordeal of finishing this book. And to all my friends, colleagues, customers, and readers . . . thank you for following my career and my continuing education.

François Payard

In my father's bakery.
A pastry chef in the making.

A Passion
for Pastry

"WHAT'S YOUR SECRET?"

People ask this of chefs all the time, and of course it is a marvelous compliment. Let me waste no time in answering that question, as it applies to desserts: If you can recognize a ripe peach, you can make a great peach tart.

It's true. If you know how to select fruit at its peak of ripeness, if you are willing to buy quality butter, quality chocolate, quality everything, and are willing to invest some time—not much time, I promise—you can make great desserts.

Growing up in a family of pastry chefs, I absorbed this lesson as unconsciously as I breathed. It took me a long time to understand that people are often intimidated by pastry and baking. And when I began to look at books on the subject, I understood why.

Many chefs concentrate too much of their efforts on making their desserts look spectacular, forgetting that flavor is primary. You have had desserts like these in restaurants, I'm sure, and also seen them in pastry books. Towers of mousse, paintings in sauce, sculptures of chocolate—all of them fun to look at, most of them tasting like . . . sculpture. To make the recipes in such books generally requires hours of your time, special skills, and a major investment in new kitchen equipment.

The pastry chefs I respect devote their skills, ingenuity, equipment, ingredients, and time to one object alone: flavor. They, and I, plan desserts that combine only as many ingredients as make sense, and we direct our staffs to chop fruit into chunks or dice it to atoms or boil it down into purées of perfect consistency. We create pastry that is paper-thin or puffy, brittle or flaky, chewy or crunchy-chewy, dry or moist. We make ice creams of seductive creaminess and intense flavor. We make chocolate dance to our tune, whether liquid or solid or something in between, like a mousse. We might add meringue, nuts or nut pastes, creams, or cookies. Then we structure each dessert, orchestrating a fragile interplay of flavor notes, choreographing textures and temperatures. We assemble these elements in a pleasing form, of course, but the dessert's complexity is, for the most part, concealed. This is what people expect in fine restaurants. This is the kind of pastry I enjoy and respect. But it is misguided, I believe, to put recipes of that nature in cookbooks and expect people at home to be able to duplicate them successfully.

To me, it is sad when someone is discouraged from trying baking and pastry making at home. As a pastry chef and a person who loves to communicate what I have learned, I was determined to create a book that would make sophisticated desserts simple to do. I wanted a variety of classic and contemporary creations, some with sleek presentation, others with fun and whimsy, and others with a rustic look. I wanted a spectrum of recipes, from the very simplest to slightly more complex, but all quite doable in a short period of time. Imagine the novelty of a French chef making things easy!

1

The basic elements that professional pastry chefs play with, and that you want to think about too, are flavor, texture, and temperature. When everything is in balance and one idea is expressed with no compromises on quality and no skimping on detail, you have a great dessert. Many chefs have grown fond of contrast and sensation—unexpected flavors in odd combinations. They get creative, and our palates suffer. Other chefs have the opposite problem: They grow timid and for the sake of "balance" will cut acidity with sweetness. It is almost a reflex, and sometimes it works, of course—but not every time.

I believe in pure flavors. I love lemon because it is tart. People rave about the lemon tart we serve in our shop, and that's because it is tart. I don't want that tartness covered or cut with too much sugar. In my shop and in the recipes in this book, we let the fruit do what it is meant to do. We layer flavor, we tantalize, we surprise, but always in the service of one main idea. Spices should complement, or support, the main flavor. A pinch of pepper, for example, can bring out the flavor of a sautéed banana. A little lemon brings out the flavor of strawberry. Salt can balance sweetness, and vanilla both complements and underlines so many flavors. It's all about bringing out the true flavors of your ingredients.

So many of the books by pastry chefs overcomplicate matters. Recipes call for homemade puff pastry, three sweet doughs, ever more sponge cakes, and temperamental custards and creams. In this book, I use only one tart shell for all the tarts, the simplest and most versatile one imaginable, and only one sponge cake, the trusty génoise. It is streamlined. But, as you can see from the Hedgehog Cake, the Bunny Cake, the Yule Logs, and many of the other desserts in this book, I enjoy decorating and having fun with my pastry. And although there are certainly some lighter desserts here, many of the recipes are rich, dense, and decadent—the Chocolate Pudding Cake, the Hazelnut Tart with Chocolate Chantilly Cream, and the Deep Chocolate Holiday Cake, to name three.

I wrote this book so I could share some of the flavor, texture, and temperature combinations that delight both me and my customers. You will find classic combinations like chocolate and hazelnut, apple and caramel, and new sensations too. You will never take figs for granted again after trying the Fig Tart, served warm with ice cream; from such simplicity, the depth of flavor is astounding. The flavor combination of apricot and raspberry in the Apricot-Almond-Raspberry Tart will create sparks in your mouth. Pecan Reine de Saba is delightfully chewy and chocolaty in the classic way, but you must also try the incredibly moist Chocolate-Pear Cake and the crumbly Sablé Breton cookies.

Every one of these recipes can be easily made in your kitchen, with ingredients found in most supermarkets and with equipment you already have. Of course, if you are just starting out, you are probably going to have to buy a few things and learn some new techniques. If you are already somewhat skilled and reasonably experienced, you will find some wonderful additions to your repertoire of desserts.

These recipes are designed to be made. Much as I love the photographs in this book, I imagine the book opened on a kitchen counter, splattered, splotched, and dog-eared.

Crazy Horse in the Kitchen

I was born in 1966 in Nice, the beautiful resort on the French Riviera. My family has owned the same pastry shop there for more than fifty years. The shop, Au Nid des Friandises, which can be translated as "the essence of sweetness," was opened by my grandfather. My mother, Denise Henry, grew up working in her father's shop. My father, Guy Payard, came to work in the shop, and that is how he met my mother.

When I was thirteen years old, my parents decided that I should work during my school vacations, and they arranged an apprenticeship with a man named Charles Ghignone. Although Chef Ghignone was sixty-five years old at the time, he was still regularly hired by all of the best resorts and hotels for weddings and special events. He created towering, intricate, delicious cakes, some of them as much as eighteen feet tall. He taught me everything about pastry and cooking.

Chef Ghignone called me *cheval fou*—crazy horse. I had too much energy and could not stand in one place. But gradually he taught me discipline, confidence, and pride in my work, and he reinforced the passion you must have to do this job well. Every year when I go back to France, I stop to say hello to Chef Ghignone. Last year, about the time of the opening of the New York shop, there was an article written about me in a French magazine. I went to see Chef Ghignone and I gave him a copy of the article. When he saw that the article referred to me as Crazy Horse, he cried for happiness.

After I left school and did my mandatory service in the army, I worked on a special culinary-themed cruise ship on the Mediterranean. That led to a position at Casino de Forges les Eaux, a restaurant and casino in Normandy, about sixty miles from Paris. Then, when I was twenty years old, I decided I was ready for Paris, and I sent out my résumé to all the great restaurants and grand hotels there.

Did some stray luck from the casino attach itself to me? I don't know, but I was able to get work in the kitchens of a string of excellent restaurants: La Tour d'Argent, Le Toit de Passy, and then Lucas Carton, which at the time was considered to be the finest restaurant in Paris, if not the world. I was only twenty-two years old when I started there. Some years later, I asked Alain Senderens, the executive chef, why he had hired me out of all the hundreds of chefs who applied for positions there every year. "Because you don't make toys," he replied, "you make food."

In 1990, I came to New York and was hired by Gilbert LeCoze, the great chef at Le Bernardin. Several years later, I went to work at Restaurant Daniel with Daniel Boulud. It quickly became one of the most popular and successful French restaurants in New York. It was during this time that I met my wife, Alexandra, and we were married in 1993. Partly through Alex's support and confidence in me, I began developing plans to open my own pâtisserie and bistro. I envisioned something that not even Paris had ever seen: a complete pâtisserie and bistro, informal yet elegant. I wanted the food to surpass anything in any Parisian bistro in quality. I wanted to sell the classic French pastries, but I wanted to have

American favorites too, and exquisite chocolates. I wanted a place that would be special but not intimidating.

Payard Pâtisserie and Bistro opened in August 1997, and today it is quite successful—it makes me uneasy to say so, but it is true. The pastries and chocolates we offer our customers disappear from the shelves, and the bistro reservation book is full most nights. We fill special orders for wedding cakes, supply other local restaurants and hotels with pastries, breads, and desserts, and take orders by mail. Some days it seems we furnish all of New York with something delicious. I didn't do it alone, of course. Chefs and cooks, designers and craftsmen, suppliers, other staff people, not to mention my wife, Alex—the list of people who have contributed to our success goes on and on . . . but it must also include the chefs I have learned from and, of course, my parents.

Four-Star Desserts in Your Home

People are fond of top ten lists, the best this, the best that. So here is a list of ten of my best-selling items in my New York bistro and shop: Lemon Tart, Rhubarb-Streusel Tart, Chocolate Tart, Hedgehog Cake, Chocolate Mikado Cake, Chocolate-Coconut Cake, Chocolate Soufflé Cake, Rhubarb-Lemongrass Soup, Strawberry Soup, and Frozen Coconut Soufflé. And you can make any of them, because the recipes are all in this book.

In creating the recipes for this book, we worked to transform four-star restaurant desserts into those that can be made in the home—reducing the number of steps involved, simplifying the ingredients and equipment required. For example, for the Chocolate Mikado Cake, in my shop, we layer hazelnut mousse and chocolate mousse on hazelnut meringue layers. Here, I have eliminated the hazelnut mousse. You still have the essential combination of hazelnut and chocolate, but there is only one mousse to make, not two. In the shop, I make a Trio of Chocolates. For this book, we have made that mousse cake into a duo. But, you can see, this is not such a difficult compromise. You still treat your family and guests to great flavor, but you won't make yourself crazy doing it.

The recipe ingredients are presented both in cup measurements and in grams. I do this because I would like to encourage people to measure by weight rather than volume. It is much more accurate, and much easier too.

Whenever I can, I give you substitutions or suggest alternatives, both for minor ingredients and major components in a recipe. This means you can make some of the recipes more convenient for you, or suit them more to your taste. But please: If there are no substitutions listed, follow the recipe exactly. Remember, baking does require precision—there is some science involved in this craft.

You will find recipes here for every occasion, inclination, and mood. Lemon Pound Cake for breakfast, Belgian Waffles for an elegant brunch, spicy Pain d'Epices for an after-school snack, moist Pineapple Tea Cakes (and a host of petits fours and cookies) to accompany tea or coffee. And, for evening and dinner parties, desserts to satisfy every taste. If you think that soufflés are impossible to do, it's only because chefs have tried to convince the world of that. They are, in fact, a snap. If you love meringue, you will love the sensation of your fork splitting its gentle layers and its crunchy sweetness against the rich chocolate ganache in Gâteau Alexandra. If you love coconut, you will want to try the Coconut-Pineapple Tart; it's like a piña colada in the form of a pastry. The flavors of moist almond cream and succulent pear are irresistible in Tarte Bourdaloue.

I've also included delicious suggestions for the holidays, including three different takes on the festive Bûche de Noël, or Yule Log, some sensuous choices for Valentine's Day, and a heavenly alternative to the Thanksgiving pecan pie—my Hazelnut Tart combines hazelnuts, chewy caramel, and flavorful clouds of chocolate chantilly. I tell you how the classic Opera Cake can be decorated to suit any occasion—birthday, Mother's Day, and more. For the weekend, there are easy loaf cakes, such as vibrant Pain d'Epices, a somewhat untraditional fruit cake. These weekend cakes will remain fresh sitting out on your kitchen counter for a few days, or in your refrigerator for a week, the perfect snack for guests, unexpected or not. On the light side (and perfect for summer too), there are dessert soups, sorbets and granités, and lighter cakes and tarts. On the not so light side, there's a whole chapter devoted to chocolate cakes. I've included many tart recipes, because they are such a simple, elegant way to present fruit in a dessert—or chocolate or even vegetables, for that matter. And my favorite ice cream recipes—caramel, praline, classic vanilla—are here too.

Even if you're a complete novice, you'll find everything you need to know to get started here. If you're not familiar with some of the ingredients or equipment in a recipe, refer to the introductory sections that explain them in detail. In the back of the book, there is a source list of companies so that you can order anything you may be missing. The book begins with some basic recipes—génoise, the classic French sponge cake; sweet tart dough; almond cream and pastry cream; and the like. These are the building blocks of pastry, and once you master them you can create so many variations. The recipes are written simply and clearly, and you should have no problems. But if you're unsure about how to proceed, scan the section on Basic Techniques, where you'll find details on how to measure ingredients, blanch and toast nuts, and so on. You'll also find some fun decorating tips: easy ways to make chocolate curls, caramel sticks, leaf decorations, and so on. Have fun, but please, no out-of-place chocolate decorations on a fruit tart. I am looking over your shoulder, just as (I feel) Chef Ghignone and my father looking over mine.

All of my life, I have had a passion for pastry. Like any great love in one's life, the feeling is unmistakable but hard to define. It touches the emotions and the intellect. It is part craft, part science, and part show business. It involves the alchemist's dexterity with chocolate; the scientist's control of temperature, leavening, crystallization; the showman's love of applause, that is, the appreciation of your customers. There's the almost child-like delight in handling a dough, and the adult's satisfaction in mastering it. There is primitive satisfaction in being a provider, and the everyday delight of finding new ways to combine flavors. I love getting up in the morning—early, I don't have to tell you—and going to work. I can spend hours in my shop on my day off and be happy. I love what I do. I hope you will enjoy one result of this passion, the book you hold in your hands. Together we will create something beautiful.

Ingredients
and Equipment

ONE FRENCH PHRASE that every serious cook should know is *mise en place*. Literally translated, it means "put in place," and it refers to the practice of arranging in the work space every ingredient and each piece of equipment necessary for a recipe before you begin. It implies, of course, that you have read through the recipe and understood it. The mise en place is an important habit to get into. Timing is so important to success in the kitchen, and having everything on hand is crucial to timing.

No doubt you already have or are familiar with most of the ingredients and equipment necessary for the recipes in this book. Here is a quick rundown, including a few special items you may not be familiar with.

Ingredients

Almond paste – A mixture of ground almonds, confectioners' sugar, and corn syrup, almond paste is available in many supermarkets. Once opened, it can be stored in the refrigerator, well wrapped in several layers of plastic, for up to six months.

Amaretto – An almond-flavored liqueur.

Apricots – Fresh apricots can be disappointingly flavorless, but if fragrant and ripe, they are wonderful. Their peak season is June and July. Ripe apricots should be somewhat firm but the flesh should feel soft when gently pressed. They can be stored in the refrigerator for three days or so.

Armagnac – A French brandy. Some of the recipes in this book call for soaking prunes in Armagnac. I like to soak them for a month, but I know this is not practical at home.

Baking powder – A leavening agent that is a mixture of baking soda, an acid (such as cream of tartar), and cornstarch, to prevent clumping. Pay attention to the sale date on any container you purchase; to test the freshness of baking powder you already have, add a teaspoonful to about ½ cup of hot water. If it bubbles, the powder is still good.

Butter – Unsalted butter, sometimes called sweet butter, is used in all the recipes in this book. (For how to make clarified butter, see page 38.) Well wrapped, butter can be stored in the freezer for up to a month.

Calvados – An apple brandy made in Calvados, in Normandy. If you can't find it, applejack is an acceptable substitute.

Chestnuts – Fresh chestnuts are in season in the fall and winter; most are imported from France. The best are firm and plump with shiny, smooth shells. The outer shell and the inner bitter skin must be removed before using the sweet meat. Unshelled nuts can be stored in a cool dry place, while shelled chestnuts must be refrigerated or frozen. Chestnuts are also available canned and vacuum-packed, as a sweetened purée, and candied. For a source for candied chestnuts and chestnut purée, see page 225.

Chocolate – In my shop, I use DGF, a French chocolate for professional kitchens. The recipes in this book were tested with Callebaut chocolate, a high-quality chocolate that is available in specialty food stores and by mail order (see Sources, page 225).

Always use the particular type of chocolate called for in a recipe. For example, do not use milk chocolate when bittersweet is called for; milk chocolate will not work the same way. The one exception: Bittersweet and semisweet chocolates can be used interchangeably. In some recipes I call for extra-bittersweet chocolate, which is now readily available in supermarkets. The extra-bittersweet contains approximately 17 percent more chocolate liquor (cocoa solids and cocoa butter) than bittersweet, and so has a deeper, richer chocolate flavor.

To store chocolate, wrap it first in plastic, then in heavy-duty aluminum foil. Ideally, chocolate should be stored in an airtight container in a cool dry place with a consistent temperature of around 65°F. Milk and white chocolates must be stored away from light because the milk solids they contain make them more perishable. Stored properly, dark and unsweetened chocolate will keep for as long as several years, milk chocolate for about one year, and white chocolate for seven or eight months.

If it is necessary to refrigerate chocolate, it should be well wrapped, as above, to prevent it from absorbing odors and protect it from moisture. When you are ready to use the chocolate, do not unwrap it until it comes to room temperature; otherwise, condensation may form on the surface, and the chocolate will seize if you try to melt it.

For information on melting chocolate and decorative work, see pages 17 to 21.

Cinnamon – I prefer cinnamon from Ceylon, which is the "real" thing (see page 226 for a mail order source). In small amounts a good-quality cinnamon from the supermarket will be fine.

Cocoa powder – Unsweetened cocoa may be alkalized (also referred to as Dutch-processed) or nonalkalized. Adding an alkali to cocoa powder helps neutralize its natural acidity. Most European cocoas are alkalized. Nonalkalized cocoa powder is lighter than alkalized, and some people feel that it has a fruity note to its flavor; alkalized cocoa has a mellower, deeper chocolate flavor.

Coconut – You will find coconut in many of the recipes in this book, because I love it—and cakes, pastries, and confections made with coconut are favorites of many of my customers too. Coconut is great because it creates balance in many of the recipes in which it is used; it brings another flavor without interfering with the sweetness or tartness of the main component. Though I occasionally use sweetened coconut, most of the recipes call for unsweetened coconut, because that way I can better control the degree of sweetness in the dessert. (They cannot be used interchangeably.) Unsweetened coconut can be found in health food stores.

Cream – For these recipes, use either heavy or heavy whipping cream, which contains 36 to 40 percent butterfat. If you can, avoid cream labeled "ultrapasteurized." That process is designed to extend shelf life but it flattens flavor and sometimes gives the cream an off taste. It's also more difficult to whip cream that has been ultrapasteurized.

Crème fraîche – A very rich, slightly fermented, thickened French cream with a delicious slightly nutty flavor. Crème fraîche is available in specialty markets and some supermarkets.

Dried fruit – Dried fruit should be somewhat moist; if it is dried out, it will not soften during baking. However, you may be able to revive it by placing it in a steamer over simmering water, or by soaking in brandy, rum, Grand Marnier, or kirsch for a minute or two. (Although you can buy dried fruit in almost any supermarket, the quality is often far better at specialty stores.)

Eggs – Grade AA large are the eggs to use in all of these recipes. In general, for baking, eggs should be brought to room temperature before using; however, it's easier to separate eggs when they are cold, so if a recipe calls for separating the yolks and whites, do that first, then bring them to room temperature. Before beating egg whites, be sure the bowl and beaters are absolutely clean and dry.

Feuilletine – Feuilletine is a relatively new addition to the pastry repertoire, used to add crunch and texture to candies, pastries, and even ice cream. We provide a mail order source on page 226, but you may wish to substitute. Traditionally made from crêpe batter, some chefs use ground corn flakes as a substitute, but I prefer Rice Krispies; they are not as sweet.

Figs – Fresh figs are in season from June through November. Look for plump fruit; figs that have begun to shrivel a bit near the stem will be particularly sweet. Often the figs you can buy are not yet ripe; allow them to ripen at room temperature until they are soft and fragrant. Ripe figs should be used as soon as possible, although they can be stored in the refrigerator for two to three days. I prefer Black Mission figs.

Fleur de sel – Literally "flower of the salt," fleur de sel is a fine sea salt with a subtle floral aroma. It is harvested only during two or three months of the year, from salt marshes in France's Brittany. For a mail order source, see page 225.

Flour – Flour provides structure in baking. Always use the flour called for in a recipe. Wheat flours contain varying amounts of gluten, a protein that gives elasticity and strength to a dough or batter, as well as certain other characteristics, such as flakiness. All-purpose flour, a blend of high-gluten (hard) and low-gluten (soft) wheats, is a flour of medium strength and gluten content of around 10 to 13 percent. Cake flour, milled from soft winter wheat, contains less gluten (about 8 percent); it is more refined than all-purpose flour and produces a soft, delicate crumb. (Do not use self-rising cake flour in these recipes.)

If cake flour is hard to find, you can make your own with all-purpose flour: For every cup of cake flour called for in a recipe, substitute a cup of all-purpose flour, but replace two tablespoons of the flour with two tablespoons cornstarch.

Ganache – A mixture of chocolate and cream made by heating cream, pouring it over chopped chocolate to melt the chocolate, and stirring until smooth, then cooling. Ganache can be used as a filling or frosting, and it is the classic truffle center.

In my shop, I make ganache a day ahead and refrigerate it overnight before using it. I've found that this extra time develops the flavor and creaminess of the ganache.

Grenadine – A red pomegranate-flavored sweet syrup, grenadine is used in both desserts and drinks. It's available at supermarkets and some liquor stores.

Instant espresso powder – Espresso powder, available in most supermarkets, is a great way to deliver intense coffee flavor without having to add too much liquid to the recipe.

Lemongrass – An herb with a fragrant sour lemon taste that is a staple of Asian cooking; in France, it is called *citronelle*. Its pale green stalks have tough outer leaves that are usually discarded, and often only the more tender lower part of the stalks are used. Fresh lemongrass is found in Asian and specialty markets; the dried has little flavor. There is no real substitute, but lemon or lime zest makes a reasonable alternative, depending on the recipe.

Mangoes – Ripe mangoes are yellow tinged with red, slightly soft to the touch, and fragrant. Peak season is May through late July. Unripe fruit should be allowed to ripen, in a plastic bag, at room temperature. Ripe mangoes can be stored in perforated plastic bags, in the refrigerator crisper, for three to five days. The flesh of the fruit must be cut away from the large flat central pit; the flesh around the pit tends to be slightly more fibrous. To remove the flesh, peel the mango and then, using a thin-bladed sharp knife, slice it off the pit. Good-quality mango purée can be purchased by mail order (see page 225).

Milk – In these recipes, milk is always whole milk.

Nut pastes – Almond paste (see page 6) is used in several of these recipes, and you will also find praline paste and pistachio paste. For recipes for praline and pistachio pastes, see page 36 and page 37. If you would prefer to purchase them, see Sources, page 225.

Nuts – The recipes in this book use hazelnuts (filberts), almonds, pecans, pistachios, and walnuts. It is crucial that nuts be fresh; because of their high oil content, they can turn rancid quickly. If you can, taste them before you buy; if they are spoiled, you will know it immediately. To keep them fresh, store nuts, well wrapped, in the refrigerator where they will keep for three months or so, or in the freezer for up to six months.

Shelled raw nuts are available natural (with skins intact) or blanched (skins removed). You can blanch nuts yourself; for blanching and toasting instructions, see page 16. Some specifics:

- I recommend almonds from California; they're the best. Almonds are available whole and sliced, either unblanched or blanched, and slivered (always blanched).

- Hazelnuts are sweet and rich and were born to be paired with chocolate.

- The best pecans are from Georgia and Texas; they're in season in the fall. I recommend you buy them in the shell; one pound of nuts will yield approximately 10 ounces of shelled pecans. Because pecans are rich and particularly high in oil, they have a tendency to turn rancid; refrigerate shelled pecans up to three months at most, or freeze for no more than six months.

- Pistachios grown in California are good, but in my opinion, Sicily's are the best in the world. You can also find good Turkish pistachios in Middle Eastern grocery stores. The red ones are dyed; try to find natural unsalted pistachios instead. Look for nuts with a slight crack in the shell; if there is no crack, it means the nuts will be soft and flavorless (and they will be almost impossible to remove from the shells).

- Walnuts in the shell should not have any cracks or holes; shelled walnuts should look plump, not shriveled.

Orange flower water – Distilled from bitter orange flowers, orange flower water is used in drinks as well as desserts.

Pastis – A licorice-flavored French apéritif. Pernod, another licorice-flavored liqueur, is available in most liquor stores and is a perfectly acceptable substitute.

Peaches – Although there is nothing like a peach at its peak of ripeness (I'm convinced they were "the food of the gods" until chocolate came along), peaches must be purchased carefully, because the flavor of an unripe peach will not much improve on ripening at home. Look for tree-ripened fruit at farmers markets. A ripe peach has a sweet smell and some tenderness when pressed. Avoid any fruit with a greenish tinge—it will never ripen. Peak season is July and August.

Pears – Pears are one of the prides of France—we grow the best. Comice pears are a French variety, as are Bosc pears. In America, I prefer to use Anjou and Bartlett pears. There is nothing better than a tree-ripened, juicy pear. But nowadays, growers tend to pick them too soon and then keep them refrigerated too long. Pears are in season from late summer through the winter, depending on the variety. When buying a pear, sniff: A ripe one emits a sweet, characteristic perfume. The flesh should have some give, but avoid pears with soft spots or other imperfections. If you are poaching the fruit, a slightly firmer one is acceptable. If you must, canned pears are quite usable in some recipes too.

Phyllo – Phyllo, or filo, is a paper-thin pastry dough. It is available frozen in many supermarkets and fresh in some specialty markets. Phyllo will keep in the refrigerator for up to a month and can be frozen for up to six months. Thaw frozen phyllo overnight in the refrigerator before using (if you thaw it at room temperature, the sheets will stick together), and don't refreeze thawed phyllo—it will be impossible to work with.

Praline paste – See *Nut pastes.*

Raspberries – Imported raspberries are now available in the dead of winter, but peak season remains late June through July, and then again from mid-September into October for late-bearing varieties. Don't buy raspberries with their hulls attached—this is an indication that they were picked too soon, and they will be tart. They can be stored in the refrigerator for up to two days. It's best not to wash raspberries at all; if you must, rinse briefly just before using and gently pat dry.

Rhubarb – Although it is usually treated as a fruit, rhubarb is actually a vegetable. Field-grown rhubarb is redder and more flavorful than the hothouse variety; peak season for field-grown rhubarb is April to June. Store rhubarb in a plastic bag in the refrigerator for no more than three days. Wash it just before using and be sure to remove any leaves; they are toxic.

Rum – I prefer Myers's dark rum for its full flavor. A light rum is used in my Mango Soup with Gingered Raspberries.

Strawberries – Like raspberries, strawberries are now available year-round, but peak season is still April through early July. In general, the smaller ones have more flavor. You can enhance the flavor of less-than-peak strawberries by sprinkling them with granulated sugar and letting them sit for a half hour or so.

Sugar – When a recipe calls for sugar, it means granulated sugar.

Vanilla – Vanilla beans have an almost intoxicating sweetness and aroma. I use vanilla beans rather than extract in most of my recipes, because they have so much flavor. In some of these recipes, the beans are used essentially whole, split lengthwise to release more flavor but the seeds left intact; in others, the seeds are scraped from the split bean (use a paring knife) and both the seeds and bean, or just the seeds, are used. The best beans are Tahitian, Madagascar (or Bourbon), and Mexican. Wrapped well in plastic, vanilla beans can be stored in a cool dry place for several months or in the refrigerator for up to six months; they can also be frozen for longer storage.

In recipes that call for vanilla extract, always use a pure extract, not imitation vanilla.

Verbena – Verbena, or lemon verbena, is an herb whose long, thin leaves have an intense lemon fragrance and flavor. It is available in specialty food markets, usually dried, but occasionally fresh.

Zest – The outer colored portion of the rind of citrus fruit. When removing zest, avoid the pith, the bitter white part of the rind. You can use a small, sharp knife or a vegetable peeler to remove strips of zest, but a zester makes it easy. You can also use a box grater for finely grated zest.

Equipment

Baking pans – Heavy-duty aluminum *cake pans* are preferable because aluminum has good heat conductivity but does not retain heat as do glass pans, which can overbake or overbrown your cakes. Light-colored pans are better than dark ones because they do not absorb too much heat. Tinned steel fluted tart pans with removable bottoms are best. A 9½-inch tart pan is the standard size, but round *tart pans* are available in a range of sizes; a rectangular (14¾ × 4½-inches) tart pan is also useful. Square tart pans are also available, but less common. All are approximately 1 inch deep. *Tartlet pans* range in size from 1¼ to 4¾ inches in diameter and ⅝ to 1¼ inches in height. Their sides are usually fluted but may be plain. As with tart pans, tartlet pans with removable bottoms are best, but the smaller sizes are only made with fixed bottoms. A *jelly-roll pan* should be made of heavy-gauge aluminum, for even heating and to prevent warping; the standard size is 10 × 15 inches. Large baking sheets are the most useful—12½ × 17½ inches. Baking sheets have sides, while cookie sheets do not. They are both fine for cookies, but a baking sheet is necessary for baking cakes.

Bowls – Stainless steel or glass mixing bowls are best. Plastic is porous and will retain odors and oils, making it unsuitable for some uses, especially whipping egg whites.

Box grater – A box grater can be used to grate chocolate for decoration and to finely grate the zest of citrus fruits. Before grating lemon or other zest, cover the fine holes of the grater with plastic wrap; when you have finished, just lift off the plastic wrap—with all the zest that usually is impossible to remove from the grater.

Cake boards – These sturdy corrugated cardboard rounds and rectangles, which come in various sizes, are used to support cakes and other desserts. They are available at specialty kitchenware shops and through mail order (see Sources, page 225). You can make your own by cutting a round or rectangle from a piece of heavy cardboard, and covering tightly with aluminum foil.

Channel knife – A channel, or cannelé, knife, also called a citrus stripper, is a small hand tool with a notched blade. It is used to remove long strips of citrus zest and to make decorative patterns on vegetables, such as cucumbers, and other fruits, as well as citrus.

Cooling racks – Rectangular or round wire cooling racks are used to support cooling baked goods in and out of the pan, allowing full air circulation around the cake or pastry.

They are also handy when glazing cakes (or pastries), because they allow the excess glaze to drip off the cake, creating a clean bottom edge.

Cutters – Round cookie or biscuit cutters and other decorative cookie cutters are used to cut out cookies, to cut cake layers into individual cakes, and to cut chocolate into different shapes for garnishes.

Double boiler – Double boilers are useful, if not essential, for melting chocolate, cooking delicate custards or curds, and other ingredients that need gentle, indirect heat. Although the standard set of nested pans is fine, most pastry chefs and other professionals prefer to use a stainless steel bowl set over a pot of hot or simmering water.

Ice cream machine – Although some granités and ices can simply be made in a home freezer, an ice cream machine is a necessity for making most frozen desserts. Machines are available in a variety of styles and models, both hand-crank and automatic, and cost anywhere from $35 to $2,000. An excellent model for the home can be obtained for as little as $400. Buy the best one you can afford.

Knives – A chef's knife is the most essential knife in the kitchen. With a long tapered blade that can range in length from 8 to 14 inches, it is suitable for a wide variety of tasks, including chopping nuts and dicing fruits. A long serrated knife is ideal for slicing a cake into layers and excellent for chopping chocolate. If the serrations are deep enough, it can be used as a decorating comb. A paring knife's easily manipulated 2- to 3-inch blade makes it useful for tasks such as peeling fruit, splitting vanilla beans, and creating garnishes.

Mandoline – A mandoline is a manually operated slicing device with an assortment of very sharp blades. There are several styles available. Some come with a set of interchangeable blades, while others have fixed but adjustable blades; some can only be used for cutting ingredients into slices of varying thicknesses, while others can be used for julienne and waffle cuts. A mandoline makes it easy to cut fruits and vegetables into uniform slices, even paper-thin if you like, and even the inexpensive models do a good job.

Measuring cups and spoons – It is essential to have separate measuring cups for dry and liquid ingredients to ensure accurate measures. Glass 1- and 2-cup measuring cups with spouts, graduated dry measuring cups, preferably metal, not plastic, and at least one set of measuring spoons (¼, ½, and 1 teaspoon and 1 tablespoon; some have ⅛-teaspoon and ½-tablespoon measures, too) are a must.

Mixer – A good heavy-duty electric mixer has a 4½- to 5-quart bowl and a paddle attachment and dough hook as well as the standard whisk attachment. I recommend the KitchenAid. Although the heavy-duty mixer has become standard equipment in many homes, most of the recipes in this book can be made with a hand-held mixer.

Molds – *Ring molds,* also called cake rings, are sturdy metal (or acrylic) rings, available in various heights and diameters. They are used for baking and assembling cakes and desserts. (See Sources, page 225.) A *charlotte mold* is a round metal mold with slightly slanted sides. Charlotte molds come in various sizes, but all are wider than they are deep.

Ovens – The temperatures and baking times given in this book are for a conventional home oven. If you are using a convection oven, reduce the temperature by 25 to 50 degrees.

Parchment paper – Parchment paper, or kitchen parchment, is useful for lining baking pans because it provides a nonstick surface. It is available in full sheet pan-sized sheets or in rolls. Triangles of parchment paper can be rolled into cones for piping chocolate and other decorating work.

Pastry bag – Pastry bags, conical bags made of canvas coated with plastic, nylon, or disposable plastic, and available in various sizes, are used for decorating and for filling pastries, cakes, cookies, and other confections. A set of plain and star tips of various sizes is essential. A St.-Honoré tip is a special tip that creates uniform oval dollops, or quenelles. Sometimes a plastic coupler may be used to attach the tips to the bag.

Pastry brushes – These are handy for applying a soaking syrup to cake layers before assembly, for brushing oil or melted butter on a pastry, such as phyllo dough, before baking, and for applying glazes to tarts and other desserts.

Pastry comb – A pastry decorating comb is a three- or four-sided scraper with a scalloped or serrated edge that is used to give a texture or pattern to the sides and/or top of a cake after frosting. It's also used to create lines or stripes in chocolate to be used for decorations or a garnish.

Plastic dough scraper – A plastic dough scraper can be used for the same tasks as a rubber spatula. It has both a flat edge and a curved edge that makes it easy to remove the last bit of batter or cream from a bowl. It covers more surface area than a rubber spatula, but it has no handle.

Ramekins – Ramekins, also known as soufflé molds or dishes, are straight-sided porcelain molds available in various sizes. The 4-ounce and 6-ounce sizes are among the most useful.

Rolling pins – Rolling pins are available in a wide range of sizes and materials: wood, plastic, metal, glass, even marble. It is useful to have two types: a hardwood broom-handle type, called a French rolling pin, which is essentially a wooden dowel 18 to 20 inches in length and about 1¼ to 2 inches thick; and a long, heavy hardwood model, sometimes called a baker's pin, which has handles, a steel rod for added weight, and a ball bearing system.

Saucepans – Heavy pans or heavy-bottomed pans are good for even heating. They should be made of a nonreactive material such as stainless steel, not aluminum.

Scales – A *balance scale,* also known as a baker's scale, is great for measuring quantities larger than an ounce, but it is large and cumbersome for home use. *Spring* and *electronic scales* are a more convenient size and are sensitive to fractions of an ounce; most of these give weights in both ounces and grams. I recommend the electronic scale for its digital readout; the better ones can be "zeroed out," meaning that you can weigh one ingredient, then return the scale to zero with the ingredient still in the bowl, and simply add the correct amount of the next ingredient—thus, you can weigh all the dry ingredients for a cake at once.

Scoops – Ice cream–type scoops with the sweep blade mechanism are useful for portioning doughs such as cookie doughs and batters as well as for serving ice creams and sorbets. They are available in round or oval shapes and in various sizes.

Spatulas – Rubber spatulas are handy for folding and mixing batters, scraping down the sides of bowls, and dozens of other tasks. They are either flat or slightly cupped and are available in rubber, plastic, or in the newer heat-resistant (up to 500°F) silicone; it's useful to have several sizes. An *offset metal spatula,* made of stainless steel, has a bend near the handle that makes it easy to spread chocolate or cake batter over a large flat area; I recommend the 12-inch length, but a small one is also useful. A long narrow *metal spatula,* or icing spatula, may be used for icing or glazing cakes and for spreading chocolate into thin sheets for creating decorations and garnishes.

Strainers and sieves – A fine strainer is essential for sauces such as crème anglaise as well as dessert soups. Most pastry chefs prefer to use fine-mesh strainers or sieves for sifting ingredients as well; and you can use either for dusting the top of a dessert with confectioners' sugar or cocoa powder.

Tart ring – A tart ring, also known as a flan ring, is a metal ring used to bake tart shells and tarts. Since it has no bottom, the ring is placed on a cookie or baking sheet and then lined with the pastry before baking. Tart rings are ¾ inch high and come in a variety of sizes; a 9-inch-diameter ring is a useful choice.

Thermometers – A *candy thermometer* is necessary to measure the temperature of cooking sugar precisely; the same thermometer can be used to check the temperature when deep-fat frying. An *instant-read thermometer* can register temperatures up to at least 220°F (some of the better digital ones register as high as 300°F) and is a good, all-purpose thermometer for baking and dessert making. Mercury *oven thermometers* are the best. Actual oven temperatures will sometimes vary from the temperature that is set, so it is a good idea to have your oven recalibrated every two to three years. Many current models allow you to recalibrate the oven yourself.

Whisks – Wire whisks are made in different shapes and sizes, suited to different functions. Large or balloon whisks are for whipping ingredients—such as egg whites—when you want to incorporate a lot of air and for folding other ingredients into these delicate mixtures. Medium to small are good for stirring or blending sauces and for combining ingredients—such as chocolate and cream for ganache—when you don't want to incorporate a lot of air.

Zester – A small tool with a handle and a blade with five holes in it, a zester is used to remove the flavorful colored outer skin of citrus fruit in thin strips, which can then be finely chopped or minced with a chef's knife if desired.

Basic Techniques and Finishing Touches

HERE ARE SOME FUNDAMENTAL TECHNIQUES you will need to prepare the recipes in this book, followed by some finishing touches—quick and easy decorations made from chocolate, caramel, tuiles, and phyllo.

Techniques

MEASURING INGREDIENTS

To measure dry ingredients with cup measures: For the recipes in this book, measure flour, cocoa, and other dry ingredients by spooning them lightly into the measuring cup and leveling the top with a spatula or the straight edge of a knife. Do not tap the measuring cup, and do not compress the ingredient.

Many professional pastry chefs measure even their liquid ingredients by weight not only because it is more accurate, but because it is easier. This is why all ingredients in my recipes are presented in grams as well as in cup measurements. I encourage you to develop the habit.

To measure liquid ingredients with cup measures: When measuring liquids in a cup, use a clear glass measuring cup that has incremental markings to the exact amount you are measuring; do not use a cup that is so large that you are forced to approximate. After pouring the liquid to that mark, place the container on the corner of a flat surface, such as a counter or table. Lean down to confirm the level. (Do not lift the container to eye level.)

BUTTERING AND FLOURING A PAN

Coat the inside of the pan evenly with butter. Sprinkle generously with flour, tilting and shaking the pan to cover it evenly. Turn the pan over and tap out the excess flour into the sink or garbage. (The butter and flour portions for the pan are not included in the ingredient amounts in the recipes.)

UNMOLDING A LOAF CAKE

Because a loaf pan is deep and narrow, it's sometimes difficult to unmold a cake baked in one. A foolproof solution is to take a rectangular piece of parchment paper and cut out a shallow triangular piece on both of the long sides. What you have left are wings, or handles. Spray the pan with nonstick spray to anchor the paper and then position the paper in the bottom of the pan, with the wings sticking up. After baking, use the wings to lift the cake from the pan.

SPLITTING A CAKE INTO LAYERS

Make sure that the cake is completely cool or it will crumble when you attempt to cut it. Use a serrated knife that is longer than the diameter of the cake. Set the cake layer on a cake-decorating stand, lazy Susan, or cardboard cake round. If a dome has formed on the cake, trim it so that it is flat. Make a vertical notch down the side of the cake (use this mark to help align the layers during assembly). To split the cake into two layers, lay one hand lightly on the top of the cake to steady it, place the knife at the midpoint of the side of the cake, and hold the knife in place while you turn the cake with the other hand to create a scored horizontal line all around it. Using this line as a guide, carefully saw straight through the cake layer. To split the cake into three layers, score two evenly spaced lines around the cake and proceed as above.

FROSTING A CAKE

Always begin with the top of the cake and finish with the sides. Once the cake is frosted, smooth the rim of frosting that will have formed around the top edge of the cake with a spatula, spreading the excess frosting in toward the center of the cake.

BLANCHING ALMONDS

To blanch almonds, place them in a pot of simmering water for about 1 minute. Using a strainer, remove them from the simmering water and place them in a bowl of cold water to cool; drain on paper towels. Pinch each nut between your thumb and index finger, and the skin will slip off. Allow the nuts to dry completely before grinding.

TOASTING NUTS AND COCONUT

Toasting brings out the full flavor of coconut and most nuts, especially almonds and hazelnuts. Do not buy preroasted nuts; the flavor will not be the same.

1. Position a rack in the center of the oven and preheat to 325°F for sliced or slivered almonds, or 350°F for whole almonds, pistachios, coconut, walnuts, hazelnuts, and pecans. Spread the nuts in a single layer on a baking sheet.

2. Toast

   sliced or slivered almonds for 5 to 10 minutes.

   whole almonds for 10 to 15 minutes.

   walnuts and pecans for 5 to 10 minutes.

   hazelnuts for 8 to 12 minutes.

   pistachios for 5 to 7 minutes.

   coconut for 6 to 10 minutes.

Shake the pan two or three times as the nuts or coconut toast. Blanched almonds and coconut will be golden when done; natural almonds will be a light brown all the way through (cut one in half to check). Hazelnuts will be fragrant and golden beneath the skins. Walnuts and pecans will likewise be fragrant.

3. Transfer the nuts or coconut to a room-temperature baking sheet to cool completely. *For unblanched hazelnuts only:* Immediately after roasting, wrap the nuts in a clean towel and let cool completely. Transfer the nuts to a large sieve and rub them back and forth against the mesh to remove the loose skins. Remove the nuts from the sieve.

MELTING CHOCOLATE

The most important thing to remember about melting chocolate is to avoid moisture: The knife used to chop the chocolate, the surface on which you are cutting, and the bowl must all be completely dry. Steam from the simmering water, a drop of water from another container, or even a too-humid environment will cause the chocolate to "seize." This is as bad as it sounds: It means the chocolate will harden to a grainy, clotted paste and become unworkable.

To melt chocolate:

1. Chop the chocolate into ½-inch pieces to maximize the surface area exposed to heat. (Milk and white chocolates do not have to be finely chopped.)

2. You can use either a double boiler or a microwave oven to melt the chocolate. The microwave oven eliminates the moisture danger of the double boiler. But if the water in a double boiler is kept below a simmer, so steam doesn't rise from it, this should not be a problem.

To melt chocolate in a microwave oven – Place the chopped chocolate in a microwave-safe container and microwave it at medium power for 1½ to 4 minutes, until the chocolate is shiny. Check often, because the chocolate will retain its shape and look solid even though it is melted. Because they are more temperamental, always stir milk and white chocolates after about 1½ minutes. (On average, 6 ounces of semisweet chocolate will require 3 minutes to melt at medium power.)

To melt chocolate in a double boiler – Place the chopped chocolate in the top of the double boiler over hot—not simmering, not boiling—water. Melt the chocolate, stirring frequently until smooth. Do not cover the bowl of chocolate while it is melting; condensation may form under the lid and drip onto the chocolate, causing it to seize. As soon as the chocolate is melted, remove the top of the double boiler from the bottom.

Milk and white chocolates melted in a double boiler must be stirred frequently, if not continually, or the milk solids will "seed"—form lumps. Stir dark chocolate frequently.

Follow the directions in the individual recipes for melting chocolate. In general, however, 1 ounce of chocolate can safely be melted with 2 ounces of a liquid such as milk, cream, liquor, coffee, or even water. To melt chocolate with a liquid, combine the chopped chocolate with the liquid and then warm them together. If you add a cold liquid to warm or warming chocolate, the liquid will harden the chocolate, and it will form gritty particles.

MAKING A PARCHMENT PAPER CONE

Cut an 8 × 12-inch rectangle of parchment paper. Cut the rectangle diagonally into two right triangles. Hold a triangle (right angle in the upper right corner) between the thumb and forefinger of your left hand, halfway down the hypotenuse. With your right hand, bring the top left corner to the top right corner, curling the paper around to form a cone. Hold the two corners together with one hand and bring the bottom corner around the cone so that all three points meet in the back. Secure the seam with two small pieces of tape. Repeat this procedure with the remaining triangle to make another cone, or save the triangle for another time.

PIPING CHOCOLATE

Be imaginative and pipe spirals, loops, jagged lines, zigzags, sunbursts, even a filigree pattern, not to mention the name and age of a birthday boy or girl.

1. Melt 2 ounces, or more, of chocolate according to the directions on page 17.

2. Stand a parchment paper cone (see above) up in a bowl of sugar or in a short narrow glass. Scrape the melted chocolate into the cone, filling it about halfway (make sure that no moisture from the pan or bowl containing the chocolate drips into the cone). Fold the open end of the cone over to seal in the chocolate. Snip the tip with sharp scissors. (Snip the tip only after you have filled the cone with chocolate, or the chocolate will start to come out as you are filling it.) If you snip off too much, the opening will be large and the chocolate hard to manage; if you snip off too little, the fine lines you produce will look awkward—unless you are a master calligrapher.

Because chocolate becomes difficult to pipe as it cools, you may want to prepare two cones and keep one warm in a low oven while you use the other. Once the chocolate in that one cools, put it in the oven to rewarm while you use the warm one.

- Practice piping on the back of a baking sheet or a sheet of wax paper. Artful piping is a matter of gaining a feel for the cone: When do you hold it vertical to the surface, and when at a diagonal? Do you hold it an inch above the dessert, or lower it until it is barely grazing the surface? You want to gain a feel, also, for maintaining the right pressure on the bag to ensure a steady flow of chocolate from the tip. You can scrape the chocolate and reuse it.

- To pipe, hold the back of the cone with your right hand (or left, if you are left-handed) so that you can pinch it with your fingers, squeezing out the chocolate. Your other hand is free to gently guide the tip of the cone.

- To finish a line, stop squeezing the cone slightly before you come to the end of the line. You can also lower the tip so that it touches the surface of the dessert just at the point you wish to stop.

$\mathcal{D}$ecorative Touches

I have noticed that people often express an interest in doing decorative touches on their desserts, but at the last minute, they think: Forget about it, it takes too much time. I promise you that these techniques are simple. You don't need a lot of skill, just a little bit of agility and a little bit of time.

Many chocolate decorations can be made with a baking sheet, either heated or cooled.

1. Warm the baking sheet over a stove burner until your basic survival instincts tell you your fingers are about to burn; this is to ensure that the chocolate can be spread in an even layer.

2. Pour melted chocolate over the back of the pan and, with an offset spatula, spread it into a thin (about ¹⁄₁₆ inch), even layer. Refrigerate until completely set, about 30 minutes, or up to several hours.

PIPED CHOCOLATE DECORATIONS

1. Pipe melted chocolate decorations onto the the back of a hot baking sheet (see above). Refrigerate.

2. When they are completely set, carefully remove the decorations with an offset spatula.

STRIPED CHOCOLATE CIGARETTES

1. Using a metal spatula, spread melted white chocolate thinly over the back of the hot baking sheet. Drag a pastry comb through the chocolate to create lines of chocolate.

2. After the white chocolate has set slightly, pour a thin layer of melted milk or dark chocolate over it. Using an offset metal spatula, smooth the chocolate into a thin layer.

3. After the chocolate has begun to set but is still pliable, form the cigarettes with a knife: Hold it at a 45-degree angle and shave the chocolate off the sheet—it will form into tight cylinders. If the chocolate is too warm, it will not curl, but rather will be gummy. Allow to cool a few moments longer. If the chocolate is too cool, it will splinter. Rewarm as necessary.

Creating chocolate cigarettes.

A CHOCOLATE NEST

Use this to hold candies at holiday time. For an interesting effect, use half white and half dark chocolate to pipe the rectangle, alternating them.

1. Place a baking sheet in the freezer for several hours.

2. Fill a parchment paper cone (see page 17) with melted chocolate. On the back of the cooled baking sheet, pipe lines of chocolate back and forth into a rectangle approximately 6 × 4 inches, making them close together. When the chocolate has just started to set, using a spatula or your fingers, roll the rectangle into a tube, overlapping so that it is firm, then quickly roll the tube into a tight circle, joining the two ends.

3. Put the nest in the refrigerator for 4 to 5 minutes to set. Sprinkle the nest with a little

Basic Techniques and Finishing Touches

confectioners' sugar if you like. Once you become proficient, you can make floral shapes. (If the nest is ruined somehow, do not remelt the chocolate and try again, as the humidity from chilling, then returning to room temperature will have affected the chocolate; start again with unused chocolate.)

Chocolate fans can be used to decorate the Chocolate Yule Log.

CHOCOLATE FANS

1. Since this is a two-hand operation, steady the baking pan against the counter or counter wall with your body.

2. Hold a metal spatula at a very slight (10-degree) angle with both hands and scrape the chocolate toward you in a fan shape. That is, move your left hand only slightly while the right hand directs the spatula to scrape the chocolate in an arc. The result should be a fan: tight pleats where the left hand acted as a fulcrum, expanding to graceful ruffles on the right.

WHITE CHOCOLATE STARS

1. Line the back of a baking sheet or pan with a piece of parchment paper. Pour melted white chocolate onto the parchment paper and, using a small offset metal spatula, spread it into a square. Place the baking sheet in the refrigerator for 10 minutes, or until the chocolate is partially set.

2. Press a 2½-inch star-shaped cutter into the chocolate to mark the outlines of as many stars as possible (do not remove the stars). Return the baking sheet to the refrigerator for at least 45 minutes, until the chocolate is completely set.

3. Press the star cutter into the outlines of the stars, then gently peel the stars off the parchment paper. The white chocolate scraps may be stored in an airtight container at room temperature and remelted.

WHITE CHOCOLATE LEAVES

1. Line the back of a baking sheet or pan with parchment paper. Melt white chocolate and add just enough green paste or liquid food coloring to tint the chocolate a pastel green, stirring until evenly blended. Transfer the chocolate to a small parchment cone (see page 17).

2. Pipe a 2- to 2½-inch-long strip of chocolate onto the prepared sheet. Pipe another strip right next to it. Using a small offset metal spatula, spread the chocolate into a rectangle about 1 inch wide, 2 to 2½ inches long, and ⅛ inch thick. Repeat to form more leaf strips. To form the leaf shapes, place the tines of a fork so that one end is in the center of the top of a chocolate strip, touching the parchment paper. Drag the fork through the chocolate, feathering it out through the outside edge of the leaf to create the jagged edge of a leaf. Repeat this motion to the bottom of the strip, then repeat on the other side of

Basic Techniques and Finishing Touches

the strip. Repeat with the remaining chocolate strips. Place the baking sheet in the refrigerator for at least 45 minutes, until the chocolate is completely set.

3. Gently peel the chocolate leaves off the parchment paper. Store in an airtight container in the refrigerator for up to five days.

STENCIL DECORATIONS

1. To create the stencil, use the plastic lid of a coffee can or other container. With a nontoxic marker, draw the form or design you wish to create. Using an X-Acto blade (available at art supply stores) or paring knife, cut out the stencil. Wash off any marker lines, then dry.

2. Place the stencil on a sheet of parchment paper. Pour melted chocolate over the stencil and spread with a spatula. Allow it to set, then carefully remove the stencil.

CHOCOLATE CURLS

1. Bring a large block of chocolate to warm room temperature, about 80°F. You can warm it to this temperature with a desk lamp, if you like; if so, keep the lamp trained on the chocolate during the procedure. (Don't try this on a humid day; it won't work.) The chocolate is ready when the surface is slightly oily but not sticky to the touch.

2. Place the chocolate in a shallow pan so that it sits snugly, and steady the pan with your body against a counter edge. Dig a potato peeler, a knife, or a melon baller into the chocolate and pull back firmly toward you. By digging deep, you will create thicker strips with not as much curl; less pressure, and you will produce thinner strips with more curl. If the chocolate is too warm, it will not curl; if it is not warm enough, it will splinter. Let it cool or rewarm as necessary.

CARAMEL

Combine ½ cup sugar with 2 tablespoons water and a pinch of salt in a medium saucepan. Cook over medium-high heat, stirring constantly and occasionally brushing down the sides of the pan with a wet pastry brush, until the sugar dissolves. Stop stirring; increase the heat to high and boil until the syrup turns to a dark amber caramel. (To avoid burns, be extremely cautious when handling hot caramel.)

CARAMEL STICKS

These can be used for decorating individual desserts, cakes, and ice cream.

1. Spray a work surface with nonstick cooking spray. Lay a sheet of parchment paper on it and smooth it against the work surface so that it sticks. (This will ensure that when the hot caramel meets the room-temperature surface, the paper won't wrinkle and ruin the effect.)

2. Make caramel (see above). Dip the end of a 1-inch-thick 5-inch-long dowel (available at hardware stores) in the hot caramel and wave it back and forth over the parchment paper, making distinct lines as straight as you can. Allow the caramel to cool.

Basic
Techniques
and
Finishing
Touches

21

3. When the caramel is completely cool, cut off the thick, accumulated ends of the caramel sticks with a knife. Gently pull the paper away from the sticks to remove them: If you wish to store them, put them in an airtight plastic container. They will keep for two weeks to a month.

CARAMEL FANS

1. Spray a work surface with nonstick cooking spray. Lay a sheet of parchment paper on it and smooth it against the work surface so that it sticks. (This will ensure that when the hot caramel meets the room-temperature surface, the paper won't wrinkle and ruin the effect.)

2. Make caramel (see page 21). Pour it into the center of the parchment paper. With a spatula, using a quick motion of your wrist, pull flare patterns of caramel out from the center, fanning it out. Do this in a circle, until you have created a sunburst. Allow to cool.

3. Cut the sunburst into various-sized fans. Gently pull the paper away from the fans to remove. Store in an airtight container for two weeks to a month.

CARAMEL FILIGREE

If you like, trace your pattern on the parchment paper, then turn it over and just trace it with the caramel. You can make any other pattern or figures you like—including numbers for a birthday cake, using the same technique.

1. Spray a work surface with nonstick cooking spray. Lay a sheet of parchment paper on it and smooth it against the work surface so that it sticks.

2. Make caramel (see page 21). Dip the end of a 1-inch-thick 5-inch-long dowel (available at hardware stores) in the hot caramel. Make a series of loops on the parchment, the first one tall and thin, the next one a little shorter and a little wider, and so on, each one returning to the same base point. Return to the base often, building up the caramel so that when it is cool the base will be solid and can be planted in the cake or other dessert.

DECORATIVE TUILES

When a baked tuile (pages 59–63) has just been taken out of the oven and is still warm, it is pliable and can be twisted and molded into various shapes to create decorative, crisp, and delicious accompaniments to creamy desserts such as ice creams, sorbets, mousses, and puddings.

For flat forms:

1. Make a stencil from a plastic coffee can lid as described on page 21.

2. Place the stencil on the prepared baking sheet. Spread the tuile batter evenly over the entire stencil and, using an offset spatula, press it firmly into the cutout. Remove the stencil and continue to make shapes with the stencil.

For three-dimensional forms:

After baking, roll the cooling tuile vertically over a rolling pin in 8-inch widths, or wind it diagonally around a dowel in half-inch widths, for a serpentine effect.

For twists or pasta-like strands:

1. Using an offset spatula, spread the tuile batter onto the prepared baking sheet in a long narrow rectangle.

2. Using a plastic comb, comb the batter, as thin as you like, in motions from left to right (not back and forth). You will end up with excess batter at both ends that will act as a frame to stabilize the entirety during baking.

3. After baking, remove the excess from both ends and cut the warm cookie into strands or twist into corkscrews.

PHYLLO FORMS

Phyllo is a great, and underrated, dough to use for decorative touches. It is so easy—all you have to do is buy it (even most professionals buy phyllo rather than make their own). Baked phyllo is ten times crisper than puff pastry, and it has such a fragile texture that you can, if you like, just break it up and sprinkle it over a creamy dessert like mousse or ice cream for some texture. Or it can be used to make a napoleon, layered with any creamy flavor components you like. I suggest mashed banana and coconut sorbet, but let your imagination run wild.

To make moons, stars, mushrooms, or other shapes:

1. Stack two or three layers of phyllo on a baking sheet, brushing each layer with clarified butter (see page 38). Chill in the refrigerator for 20 minutes.

2. Preheat the oven to 350°F.

3. Cut the phyllo into shapes as you need them and remove the scraps. Lay a second baking sheet on top of the phyllo cutouts to keep them flat and bake for 10 to 12 minutes, until they are a light brown.

You can mix one part cocoa powder with three parts clarified butter before brushing it onto the phyllo to make chocolate phyllo. Or mix one part clarified butter with two parts of honey and brush it on the phyllo; the result will be just as crisp as phyllo brushed only with butter, but will have a wonderful flavor. Store in an airtight container for one or two days.

CANDIED LEAVES AND FLOWER PETALS

People always notice how beautiful a decorative leaf is on a yule log or other cake, and they are surprised at how delicious it is when they eat it, but they never guess how simple it is to do. You can use mint, rose petal, violet, tarragon, verbena, cilantro, chives, basil—any edible leaves. I love them because the flavor is so distinct.

1. Preheat the oven to 200°F. Line a baking sheet with parchment paper.

2. Dip each leaf in beaten egg whites and shake off the excess. Dip in sugar, turning to coat both sides, and place on the baking sheet. Allow to dry in the oven for 3 to 4 hours, or until thoroughly dry and crisp. Store in an airtight container for up to a month.

Assembling my chocolate showpiece for the first chocolate show in New York.

Pastry Basics

The recipes in this book are based on the fundamental components found in this section. To make your life simpler, I have included only one basic cake recipe and one tart shell recipe. Both are easy and versatile.

With these building blocks, you can create your own desserts too, as simple or elaborate as you wish.

Sweet Tart Dough

*T*his recipe for the rich, sweet short dough known as pâte sucrée is the only one you will need for the tarts in this book. In addition to its use as the pastry shell for tarts and tartlets, pâte sucrée is frequently used in petits fours, for filled cookies, and as a thin sweet crust under mousse desserts. This recipe makes enough pastry for two tart shells. You can freeze half for another time, or you can roll out and shape both shells and freeze one of them, well wrapped, ready to use.

MAKES TWO 9½-INCH
TART SHELLS

1 cup plus 1 tablespoon (122 grams) confectioners' sugar

1¾ cups (254 grams) all-purpose flour

Pinch of salt

9 tablespoons (127 grams) unsalted butter, softened

1 large egg

1. Sift together the confectioners' sugar, flour, and salt into a bowl.

2. Place the butter in a food processor and process until smooth, about 15 seconds. Scatter the flour mixture over the butter, add the egg, and process just until the dough forms a mass; do not overmix. Turn the dough out onto the counter and divide it in two. Shape each half into a disc, wrap in plastic wrap, and refrigerate for at least 2 hours or up to 24 hours. Half of the dough may be well wrapped and frozen for up to 1 month.

3. Let the dough stand at room temperature for 30 minutes to soften. Lightly butter two 9½-inch fluted tart pans with removable bottoms.

4. Dust a work surface lightly with flour. Dust one of the discs lightly with flour and, using a floured rolling pin, roll it out into a rough 12-inch circle. Lift the dough often, making sure that the work surface and dough are lightly floured at all times. Roll the dough up onto the rolling pin and gently unroll it over one of the prepared tart pans. Press the dough into the pan and roll the pin over the top of the pan to remove the excess dough. Repeat with the remaining dough and tart pan. Prick the bottom of the tart shells all over with a fork. Chill the tart shells for 20 minutes. (The tart shells can be refrigerated for up to 24 hours.)

TO PARTIALLY BAKE THE TART SHELLS

Preheat the oven to 325°F. Lightly butter two pieces of aluminum foil large enough to generously line each tart pan. Line the tart shells with the foil, buttered side down, and fill with dried beans, rice, or pie weights.

Bake the tart shells for 15 minutes. Remove the foil and beans and continue baking for 5 minutes, until just set; the tart shells should have little or no color. Cool completely on a wire rack.

TO PREBAKE THE TART SHELLS

Preheat the oven to 325°F. Lightly butter two pieces of aluminum foil large enough to generously line each tart pan. Line the tart shells with the foil, buttered side down, and fill with dried beans, rice, or pie weights.

Bake the tart shells for 15 minutes. Remove the foil and beans and continue baking for 8 to 10 minutes longer, until evenly golden brown. Cool completely on a wire rack.

Génoise

4 large eggs

½ cup plus 1 tablespoon (112 grams) sugar

¾ cup plus 1 tablespoon (105 grams) cake flour, sifted

2 tablespoons (28 grams) unsalted butter, melted

1. Preheat the oven to 350°F. Butter a 9-inch round cake pan. Dust the pan with flour and tap out the excess.

2. Fill a medium saucepan one-third full with water and bring to a simmer. Whisk together the eggs and sugar in the bowl of an electric mixer until combined. Place the bowl over the pan of simmering water and whisk constantly until the egg mixture is warm to the touch. Transfer the bowl to the mixer stand and beat on high speed until the mixture has tripled in volume and forms a thick ribbon when the whisk is lifted, about 5 minutes. Using a rubber spatula, fold in the flour just until blended. Fold in the melted butter, being careful not to deflate the batter.

3. Scrape the batter into the prepared cake pan and bake for 20 to 25 minutes, until the génoise is golden brown and springs back when lightly touched. Let the cake cool in the pan on a rack for 10 minutes, then unmold and cool completely right side up on the rack.

Génoise is our sponge cake of choice. Light and airy, it is firmer and dryer than the sponge cakes most Americans are familiar with. Still, this recipe makes a génoise that is very moist. One reason I prefer it is that it is so versatile. It is great for layer cakes, it takes the addition of finely ground nuts and zests and liquors very well, and it is ideal for brushing with a flavored soaking syrup.

MAKES ONE 9-INCH ROUND CAKE

Pastry Basics

Pastry Cream

*P*astry cream, or *crème pâtissière,* is the classic filling for eclairs, cream puffs, and French fruit tarts, and it's used in many other desserts, including warm soufflés. It can be flavored in a variety of ways (liqueurs are a common option), but chocolate (see Chocolate Yule Log, page 196) and coffee are especially popular.

MAKES ABOUT 2⅓ CUPS

2 cups (484 grams) whole milk

1 vanilla bean, split (see Note)

½ cup (100 grams) sugar

⅓ cup (40 grams) cornstarch, sifted

6 large egg yolks

2 tablespoons (28 grams) unsalted butter

1. Line a shallow baking pan (such as a 9-inch square pan) with plastic wrap. Put the milk in a medium saucepan, scrape the seeds from the vanilla bean into the pan, and add the bean. Bring to a boil and remove from the heat.

2. Whisk together the sugar and cornstarch in a small bowl. Place the yolks in a medium bowl; whisk in the sugar mixture and whisk until the mixture turns pale yellow and is thick and smooth. Gradually pour half of the hot milk into the yolk mixture and whisk to combine. Return the mixture to the saucepan and cook over medium heat, whisking constantly, until the mixture thickens and comes to a boil. Boil for several seconds, then remove the pan from the heat and whisk in the butter until completely melted.

3. Scrape the pastry cream into the prepared pan, spreading it evenly with a rubber spatula. Cover the pastry cream with plastic wrap, placing it directly against the surface to prevent a skin from forming. Refrigerate until needed, or up to 3 days. Remove the vanilla bean before using the pastry cream.

NOTE: If you don't have a vanilla bean, whisk in 1 teaspoon pure vanilla extract with the butter.

Almond Cream

1¼ cups (250 grams) sugar

2 cups (240 grams) slivered almonds

17 tablespoons (2 sticks plus 1 tablespoon) (241 grams) unsalted butter, softened

2 large eggs

1 large egg yolk

1 tablespoon (9 grams) all-purpose flour

1. Place ¼ cup (50 grams) of the sugar and the almonds in the bowl of a food processor and process until finely ground, about 1 minute.

2. In the bowl of an electric mixer fitted with the paddle attachment, beat the butter and the remaining 1 cup (200 grams) sugar on high speed until well combined, about 1 minute. Add the ground almond mixture and mix on low speed until combined. Add the eggs and egg yolk one at a time, beating well after each addition and scraping down the side of the bowl as necessary, then beat on medium-high speed until light and fluffy, about 3 minutes. Mix in the flour until just combined. Store in an airtight container in the refrigerator for up to a week, or freeze for up to a month.

*A*lmond cream, or frangipane, is used as a filling in cakes, tarts, and petits fours. Its flavor complements chocolate, fruits, and other nuts. When the cream is baked, it becomes somewhat cakey, but it also adds moisture to the dessert's texture. This recipe makes four cups, a large amount, but, sealed tightly in a plastic container, almond cream can be stored in the refrigerator for up to a week and frozen for up to a month.

MAKES ABOUT 4 CUPS

*Pastry
Basics*

Vanilla Buttercream

*T*here are many recipes for buttercream. I prefer this classic French version made with whole eggs and a sugar syrup. Rich, creamy, and delicious, it can be stored in the refrigerator for up to one week, but be sure to bring it to room temperature before using.

MAKES ABOUT 6 CUPS
(enough to fill and frost two 9-inch round layer cakes)

Special Equipment:
Candy Thermometer

5 large eggs

2 cups (400 grams) sugar

1¼ pounds (5 sticks) (567 grams) unsalted butter, softened

1 teaspoon (4 grams) pure vanilla extract

1. In the large bowl of an electric mixer, using the whisk attachment, begin beating the eggs on medium speed.

2. Meanwhile, combine the sugar and ⅓ cup (78 grams) water in a medium saucepan. Bring to a boil over medium-high heat, stirring to dissolve the sugar. Insert a candy thermometer into the pan and cook until the syrup reaches 243°F. With the mixer running, immediately pour the hot syrup down the side of the bowl into the eggs (avoid pouring the syrup onto the whisk, or it will splatter). Increase the speed to medium-high and continue beating until the eggs are cool and have doubled in volume, about 7 minutes.

3. Beat in the softened butter 1 tablespoon at a time (see Note). Increase the speed to high and beat until the buttercream is shiny and smooth, about 2 minutes. Beat in the vanilla extract. The buttercream can be used right away or placed in an airtight container and refrigerated. Bring to room temperature and beat with a whisk until smooth before using.

MOCHA BUTTERCREAM
Dissolve 2 tablespoons (4 grams) instant espresso powder or instant coffee in 1 tablespoon (15 grams) hot water. Beat into the finished buttercream.

NOTE: Buttercream sometimes has a tendency to curdle. Here is a trick you can use to rescue it if the buttercream mixture should appear separated at any point while you are adding the butter. Stop beating the buttercream and heat 2 tablespoons (29 grams) of heavy cream in a small saucepan. Whisk the hot cream into the buttercream to bring it together, then continue adding the butter.

Crème Anglaise

1 cup (242 grams) whole milk

1 cup (232 grams) heavy cream

1 vanilla bean, split

5 large egg yolks

½ cup (100 grams) sugar

This rich custard sauce is the perfect accompaniment to many of the cakes, tarts, and soufflés in this book. Crème anglaise is also the base for French ice creams. Pay attention to the physical cues of doneness: It is far too easy to overcook crème anglaise, and you will end up with "scrambled" eggs. If possible, chill it for at least twenty-four hours before using to intensify the flavor.

MAKES ABOUT 2¼ CUPS

1. Combine the milk and cream in a medium saucepan, scrape the seeds from the vanilla bean into the pan, and add the bean. Bring to a boil over medium heat. Remove from the heat, cover, and let stand for 10 minutes.

2. Half-fill a large bowl with cold water. Add two large handfuls of ice cubes and set this ice bath aside.

3. Whisk together the egg yolks and sugar in a medium bowl. Gradually whisk in ½ cup of the warm milk mixture until well blended. Pour this mixture back into the saucepan. Cook over medium-low heat, stirring constantly with a wooden spoon, for 2 to 3 minutes, or until the custard is thick enough to coat the back of the spoon; do not let the sauce boil. Immediately pour the sauce through a fine-mesh sieve into a medium bowl and place the bowl in the ice bath (add a few more ice cubes if necessary). Stir occasionally until the sauce is completely cool. Cover the sauce with plastic wrap and refrigerate for several hours, until well chilled, or, preferably, overnight. Remove the vanilla bean before serving.

Chocolate Sauce

This sauce is a classic ganache—equal proportions of chocolate and cream—thinned with a little water. Serve it warm to accompany the Chocolate-Pear Cake (page 93).

MAKES ABOUT 1¾ CUPS

8 ounces (227 grams) bittersweet chocolate, finely chopped
1 cup (232 grams) heavy cream
1 teaspoon (4 grams) pure vanilla extract

Put the chocolate in a medium bowl. Combine the cream and ½ cup (118 grams) water in a medium saucepan, and bring to a boil over medium-high heat. Pour over the chocolate and gently whisk until the chocolate is completely melted and the sauce is smooth. Whisk in the vanilla. Serve warm. The sauce can be made up to 1 week ahead. Let cool to room temperature before storing in an airtight container in the refrigerator. Reheat in a heavy saucepan over low heat.

Chocolate Glaze

Chocolate glaze is used to add a little flavor and a sleek (Chocolate Mikado Cake, page 105), or rustic, appearance to cakes and other pastries, depending on how it is applied. The addition of corn syrup makes this glaze particularly easy to work with and helps keep it shiny.

MAKES ABOUT 2¼ CUPS

12 ounces (340 grams) bittersweet chocolate, finely chopped
1 cup (232 grams) heavy cream
½ cup (164 grams) light corn syrup

Put the chocolate in a medium bowl. Combine the cream and corn syrup in a small saucepan and bring to a boil over medium-high heat. Pour over the chocolate and, using a rubber spatula, stir until the chocolate is completely melted and the glaze is smooth. Use the glaze warm or store, covered, in the refrigerator for up to 3 days. Reheat the glaze in a bowl over barely simmering water or in the microwave at medium power for 1 to 2 minutes, stirring once or twice.

Pastry Basics

Apricot Glaze

Apricot glaze adds sheen and a subtle flavor to many French tarts and cakes. It also helps keep them moist.

MAKES ABOUT ¼ CUP

⅓ cup (95 grams) apricot preserves

Place the preserves in a small heatproof glass measure and microwave on high power for 30 to 45 seconds, until bubbling. Strain the hot preserves through a fine-mesh sieve into a small bowl. Use the glaze warm.

Strawberry Marmalade

Most marmalades are made from citrus fruits. I like to use this chunky strawberry marmalade as a filling, and it's an excellent accompaniment to some of the soufflés. Adding lemon zest really brings out the strawberry flavor.

MAKES ABOUT 2 CUPS

1 pint (226 grams) ripe strawberries, washed, hulled, and cut into quarters

2 tablespoons (25 grams) sugar

Grated zest of 1 lemon

Combine the strawberries and sugar in a medium saucepan. Cook over medium heat, stirring constantly, but trying not to break up the strawberries, until the sugar is dissolved and some of the liquid from the berries is released, about 3 minutes. When the mixture boils, remove it from the heat and stir in the lemon zest. Let the marmalade cool to room temperature, then refrigerate in an airtight container until needed, or up to 3 days.

Poached Pears

The pear is the perfect medium to absorb the flavors of so many liquids. It retains its "pearness" as it gains flavor— just about any flavor you want. Wines and liqueurs, such as crème de cassis, are typical, but you can use your imagination. The important point in poaching is to lower the heat and cook below the boiling point so that the pears retain their shape.

MAKES 6 PEAR HALVES

1 tablespoon (16 grams) fresh lemon juice

¼ cup (50 grams) sugar

1 vanilla bean, split

3 large (794 grams) ripe but firm pears, such as Anjou or Bartlett, peeled, halved, and cored

Combine 4 cups (944 grams) water, the lemon juice, and sugar in a medium saucepan. Scrape the seeds from the vanilla bean into the pan and add the bean. Heat over medium-high heat, stirring, until the sugar dissolves. Add the pears and bring to a boil. Cover the pan and simmer over low heat for 10 to 12 minutes, or until the pears are tender when pierced with a fork. Remove the pan from the heat and cool, covered. Refrigerate the pears in their liquid until ready to use, or up to 3 days.

Pastry
Basics

Meringue Mushrooms

2 large egg whites, at room temperature

2 teaspoons (10 grams) fresh lemon juice

⅔ cup (133 grams) sugar

Unsweetened alkalized cocoa powder for dusting

*M*eringue mushrooms are the classic garnish to a yule log (see pages 196 and 201 for recipes). They add a whimsical mood and visual depth when placed sparingly at the base of these "log" cakes. The dusting of cocoa is intended to give them an "earthy" look.

MAKES ABOUT THIRTY 1½-INCH MUSHROOMS

Special Equipment:
Pastry Bag Fitted with a ⅜-Inch Plain Tip (Such as Ateco #4)

1. Preheat the oven to 225°F. Line a large baking sheet with parchment paper.

2. In the bowl of an electric mixer, using the whisk attachment, beat the egg whites at medium-low speed until foamy. Add the lemon juice and beat at medium speed until the whites begin to form soft peaks. Add the sugar one third at a time, then increase the speed to high and beat until stiff peaks form.

3. Fill a pastry bag fitted with a ⅜-inch plain tip with the meringue. To pipe the caps, hold the pastry bag upright with the tube slightly above the prepared baking sheet and squeeze the bag with a steady, even pressure, gradually raising the tube as the meringue begins to build up but keeping the tip buried in the meringue, until the cap is about 1½ inches in diameter. Once it is the right size, stop applying pressure to the bag and remove the tip from the meringue; use the tip to smooth out the point in the cap. Form 30 caps, spacing them about ¾ inch apart, on one half of the baking sheet. Sift a light dusting of cocoa powder over the caps.

4. To form the stems, on the other half of the baking sheet, hold the bag perpendicular to the sheet with the tube touching it and squeeze hard, keeping the tip buried in the meringue, until you have formed a ¾-inch-high cone. Make 30 stems. Reserve the remaining meringue at room temperature.

5. Bake the caps and stems for 40 to 45 minutes, or until firm to the touch. Leave the oven on.

6. Using a pastry tip or small knife, make a small hole in the underside of each cap. Fill each hole with a small mound of the reserved meringue. Set the caps over the points of the stems and bake for an additional 30 minutes, or until the mushrooms are thoroughly dry. Store the mushrooms in an airtight container for up to 2 months.

Pastry Basics

Praline Paste

*P*raline is basically a nut brittle, classically made with almonds and caramelized sugar. I like to use a combination of buttery hazelnuts and almonds and even add some fragrant hazelnut oil. Ground into a paste, praline makes a rich, very flavorful addition to cakes, candies, ice creams, soufflés, and other desserts.

MAKES 1 GENEROUS CUP

½ cup (70 grams) blanched almonds

½ cup (71 grams) blanched hazelnuts

¾ cup (150 grams) sugar

1 vanilla bean, split

1 tablespoon (13 grams) hazelnut oil (see Note) or vegetable oil

1. Preheat the oven to 350°F.

2. Spread the almonds and hazelnuts on a baking sheet and toast in the oven for 8 to 12 minutes, shaking the pan once or twice, until golden and fragrant. Transfer the nuts to a room-temperature baking sheet to cool completely.

3. Brush another baking sheet lightly with vegetable oil. Combine the sugar and 2 tablespoons (30 grams) water in a medium heavy saucepan. Scrape the seeds from the vanilla bean into the pan (save the pod for another use) and bring to a boil over medium-high heat, stirring to dissolve the sugar. Continue to cook, without stirring, until the mixture turns a light caramel, 3 to 5 minutes. Remove the pan from the heat and stir in the toasted almonds and hazelnuts. Return the pan to the heat and cook, stirring, until the nuts are completely coated with the caramel and it deepens to an amber color. Immediately pour the caramelized nut mixture onto the oiled baking sheet. (To avoid burns, be extremely cautious when handling hot caramel.) Allow the praline to cool for 30 minutes, or until hard.

4. Using a large knife, coarsely chop the praline. Place in a food processor and process for about a minute, until the consistency of sand. Add the hazelnut oil and process for another 30 seconds, or until it becomes a paste. Store in an airtight container in the refrigerator for up to a week.

NOTE: Hazelnut oil is available at specialty gourmet markets; for a mail order source, see page 225.

Pistachio Paste

1¼ cups (190 grams) shelled pistachio nuts

¾ cup (150 grams) sugar

1 vanilla bean, split

8 mint leaves

2 tablespoons (27 grams) vegetable oil

*T*his variation on praline paste adds moisture, flavor, and crunch to ice creams, cakes, and candies. I add mint because it brings out the flavor of pistachio, and it enhances the color as well.

MAKES ABOUT 1⅔ CUPS

1. Preheat the oven to 350°F.

2. Spread the pistachio nuts on a baking sheet and toast in the oven for 5 to 7 minutes, shaking the pan once or twice, until fragrant. Transfer the nuts to a room temperature baking sheet to cool completely.

3. Brush another baking sheet lightly with vegetable oil. Combine the sugar and 2 tablespoons (30 grams) water in a medium heavy saucepan. Scrape the seeds from the vanilla bean into the pan (save the pod for another use) and bring to a boil over medium-high heat, stirring to dissolve the sugar and brushing down the sides of the pan with a wet pastry brush. Continue to cook, without stirring, until the mixture turns a light caramel, 3 to 5 minutes. Remove the pan from the heat and stir in the toasted pistachios and mint leaves. Return the pan to the heat and cook, stirring, until the nuts are completely coated with the caramel and it deepens to an amber color. Immediately pour the caramelized nut mixture onto the oiled baking sheet, separating the nuts a bit with a wooden spoon so they are not mounded. (To avoid burns, be extremely cautious when handling hot caramel.) Allow the pistachio praline to cool for 30 minutes, or until hard.

4. Using a large knife, coarsely chop the praline. Place in a food processor and process for about a minute, until the consistency of sand. Add the vegetable oil and process for about 30 seconds longer, until it becomes a paste. Store in an airtight container in the refrigerator for up to 1 week.

Pastry
Basics

37

Simple Syrup

This classic syrup is used as a base for sauces and sorbets and for brushing génoise layers. By increasing or reducing the proportion of sugar to water, it can be made thicker or thinner, depending on what you will be using it for; this version is thin enough to be perfect for soaking génoise.

MAKES ABOUT 2¼ CUPS

2½ cups (500 grams) sugar

Combine the sugar and 1 cup (236 grams) water in a medium nonreactive saucepan and bring to a boil over medium-high heat, stirring to dissolve the sugar. When the sugar is completely dissolved, pour the syrup into a bowl and let cool to room temperature. Store in an airtight container in the refrigerator for up to 2 weeks.

Clarified Butter

Clarifying butter is a process of removing the milk solids from butter. Clarified butter has a much higher smoking point than regular butter (it is the milk solids that burn during sautéing). To finish with the amount of clarified butter you need, start with about 33 percent more unsalted butter than that amount. (For example, if you want six tablespoons of clarified butter, start with eight tablespoons of butter.)

Have a fine-mesh sieve ready, or line a coarser sieve with a layer of cheesecloth. Cut the butter into tablespoons and melt in a heavy saucepan over medium heat; do not stir. Continue to cook until the solids drop to the bottom of the pan and begin to turn brown. When the bubbling subsides, strain the butter through the sieve. Clarified butter will keep for months in an airtight container in the refrigerator.

Dessert Soups

*U*ntil recently, fruit soups were much more popular in Europe—where they are often served as a digestif, or a small course to refresh the palate and aid digestion before the "main" dessert—than in the United States. Now, many restaurants here are serving dessert soups, and so are people at home. At Restaurant Daniel, we served fifteen or twenty different soups, either as a "pre-dessert" or as a light dessert course on its own. Fruit soups are more interesting and more elaborate than sorbets, and more appealing than fruit plates.

Each of these soups is refreshing, flavorful, and, of course, very light. They are easy to make, with no special equipment necessary. Shopping is easy too, because they are designed to take advantage of whatever fruit is in season. I recommend that you place a small scoop of sorbet in the center of each serving bowl and then ladle the soup around the sorbet, and I offer suggestions for the appropriate sorbet to serve with each soup. Dried fruit chips, such as apple, banana, or apricot chips, can be used as a garnish for some texture. Don't serve these soups with petits fours or cookies; their sweetness will distort your palate's appreciation of the fruit flavor. Some of these soups are meant to take advantage of winter citrus and would be ideal after a hearty meal, but, of course, a cold fruit soup is tailor-made for summer.

I've also included two recipes for dessert "fricassees." The word *fricassee* usually refers to a meat dish; the classic example, of course, is chicken, sautéed in butter, then stewed with vegetables and, usually, wine. These dessert fricassees, like their savory counterparts, are more stew than soup, with large chunks of fruit or even whole fruits. Because they are more substantial than most fruit soups, I serve them with a scoop of ice cream, rather than sorbet.

Dessert soups can be made one to two days in advance of serving, but they should be garnished right before serving. The fricasees should be made right before serving, in order to take advantage of the fresh flavors and textures.

Spiced Cherry Soup

I look forward to summer every year, and one reason is cherries. They are so delicious and so confounding—cherry pie aside, sometimes people don't know what to do with them, especially sour cherries. This soup is a great way to use sour cherries, but if you don't like their tartness, you can use either sweet black cherries or white cherries. I don't recommend mixing them; the color of the soup will be unappealing. Serve with Strawberry Sorbet (page 182), if desired.

MAKES 8 SERVINGS

Flavor Sachet

1 cinnamon stick

1 star anise

1 whole clove

Grated zest of 1 lime

Grated zest of 1 lemon

Grated zest of 1 orange

Soup

1½ pounds (680 grams) fresh cherries, pitted

¾ cup (150 grams) sugar

Garnish

1 pound (453 grams) fresh cherries, pitted and cut in half, or into thirds if large

8 mint sprigs

1. *Make the flavor sachet:* Place the cinnamon stick, star anise, clove, and citrus zests in the center of a 4-inch square of cheesecloth. Bring the corners of the cloth together to form a pouch and tie it securely with kitchen string; set the sachet aside.

2. *Make the soup:* Combine the cherries, 3¼ cups (767 grams) water, and the sugar in a large saucepan and bring to a boil, stirring occasionally. Remove the pan from the heat and add the flavor sachet. Cover the pan and let stand for 2 hours to blend and bring out the flavors.

3. Remove the sachet from the soup. Pour the soup into a food processor or blender and process until smooth. Strain the soup through a sieve into a large bowl. Refrigerate for at least 3 hours, or until thoroughly chilled.

4. *Serve the soup:* Pour the soup into bowls and garnish with the cherries and mint sprigs.

Strawberry Soup

Soup

1 tablespoon plus 1 teaspoon (17 grams) liquid pectin, optional (see Note)

½ cup (100 grams) sugar

Grated zest of 1 lemon

1 stalk lemongrass, chopped, or grated zest of 1 lime

2 quarts plus 1 cup (1 kilo) strawberries, washed, hulled, and quartered

Grated zest of 1 lime

Garnish

6 strawberries, washed and hulled

8 mint sprigs

1. *Make the soup:* Combine 1⅔ cups (391 grams) water, the pectin, if using, the sugar, lemon zest, and lemongrass in a medium saucepan and cook over medium-high heat, stirring constantly, until the sugar dissolves. Increase the heat to high and bring the mixture to a boil. Remove the pan from the heat.

2. Place the quartered strawberries in a medium bowl. Set a sieve over it and pour the hot lemongrass liquid through the sieve. Add the grated lime zest, cover the bowl with plastic wrap, and refrigerate for at least 8 hours, or overnight.

3. *Make the garnish:* thinly slice the strawberries lengthwise. Stack the slices, a few at a time, on top of each other and cut into thin strips.

4. *Serve the soup:* Arrange the quartered strawberries in eight shallow bowls. Pour the soup through a sieve over the fruit. Garnish the soup with the strawberry strips and mint sprigs.

NOTE: Pectin is available in most supermarkets.

Union Square Greenmarket is located, oddly but wonderfully, in the middle of New York City. I was shopping there one morning and found plump wild strawberries, right from the farm. With amazing flavor, they were as good as, if not better than, the ones grown in France, and I immediately began to conceive a strawberry soup in my imagination. Although this soup is best when strawberries are in season, it will work year-round; what you will lose is the great, fiery color. I add lemon, which rounds out the flavor; lemongrass, which gives a slight Asian spice accent to the soup; and lime—every berry needs a little lime to bring its flavor properly to the palate. If you can't find lemongrass, you can replace it with lime zest. Serve this with Strawberry Sorbet (page 182).

If you want a slightly thicker soup, use the optional liquid pectin.

MAKES 8 SERVINGS

*Dessert
Soups*

Red Wine Soup

When I was a kid, my parents would sometimes serve us hot wine and peaches. Although that was the inspiration for this soup, the secret ingredient is the tea bag. Though I was envisioning a sangria lightness for this soup, I knew I had to start with a heavy-bodied wine, because I would need to boil it to remove much of the alcohol. Beaujolais is very fruity, but it has no body; I suggest a Cabernet. I added cloves, some berries, strawberries, and pineapple. (This recipe is a good way to use up berries that are going soft.) When I tasted the result, I realized something was missing, so I added a tea bag, which gave an amazing flavor to the wine. Use Earl Grey or a flavored tea, any flavor you like. You can serve this soup in a bowl, of course, but for more panache, try it in a stemmed wine glass, perhaps with a strawberry floating, or layered with ice cream and sliced peaches, like a parfait. The soup also works as a sauce, poured over vanilla ice cream or peaches, or both.

MAKES 8 SERVINGS

Dessert
Soups

Soup

4 cups (936 grams) full-bodied red wine, such as Cabernet

2 black peppercorns

1 cinnamon stick

Grated zest of 2 oranges

Grated zest of 1 lemon

¼ pineapple, peeled, cored, and diced

10 large strawberries, washed, hulled, and cut into quarters

1 berry-flavored tea bag

Garnish

½ pint (227 grams) fresh berries, such as raspberries, strawberries, or blackberries

8 mint sprigs

1. *Make the soup:* Combine the red wine, peppercorns, cinnamon stick, and orange and lemon zests in a medium saucepan, and bring to a boil over medium-high heat. Boil until reduced by one third, about 10 minutes. Remove the pan from the heat and add the pineapple, strawberries, and tea bag. Allow the mixture to stand for 5 minutes.

2. Remove the tea bag, transfer the soup to a medium bowl or pitcher, and refrigerate for at least 3 hours, until well chilled. Strain the soup through a sieve and refrigerate until serving time.

3. *Serve the soup:* Ladle or pour the soup into shallow soup bowls and garnish each with a few berries and a mint sprig.

Watermelon Soup

Flavor Sachet
Grated zest of 1 lime

Grated zest of 1 orange

One 1-inch piece (12 grams) ginger, sliced

½ vanilla bean, split

Pinch of Chinese 5-spice powder

Soup
½ (about 10 pounds) (4.5 kilos) large watermelon

½ cup (100 grams) sugar

Garnish
6 mint sprigs

1. *Make the flavor sachet:* Place the lime zest, orange zest, ginger, vanilla bean, and 5-spice powder in the center of a 3-inch square of cheesecloth. Bring the corners of the cloth together to form a pouch and tie it securely with kitchen string. Set the sachet aside.

2. *Make the soup:* Place the watermelon half, cut side up, on a large baking sheet (to catch the juices). Using a paring knife and angling it slightly toward the center, cut a 2-inch-wide by 2-inch-deep 14-inch-long rectangle of watermelon flesh from the center of the melon. (This piece should be almost seedless.) Dice this piece, discarding any seeds, and reserve it in a covered bowl in the refrigerator to garnish the soup.

3. Cut the melon in half lengthwise. Remove the remaining watermelon flesh, cut it into chunks, and transfer it and any juice to a blender or food processor (don't worry about the seeds). Process until slushy, about 30 seconds. Strain the watermelon slush through a fine-mesh sieve into a 2-quart glass measure or a medium bowl. Cover and refrigerate for at least 4 hours or up to 24 hours.

4. Combine ½ cup (118 grams) water and the sugar in a medium saucepan and bring to a boil, stirring to dissolve the sugar. Remove the pan from the heat and add the flavor sachet. Cover the pan and allow the flavors to infuse for 2 hours.

5. Remove the sachet from the sugar syrup, transfer the syrup to a medium bowl or large pitcher, and refrigerate until cold, about 1 hour.

6. Stir the watermelon slush well until blended. Stir 2 cups of the slush into the cooled syrup and refrigerate until chilled, about 2 hours.

7. *Serve the soup:* Scatter the reserved diced watermelon in the bottom of six shallow soup bowls. Pour the soup over the fruit and garnish with the mint sprigs.

*W*atermelon's elusive flavor is gently spiked with a sachet of lime zest, orange zest, ginger, vanilla, and Chinese 5-spice powder. The soup that results is unmistakably watermelon, with a subtle sizzle. When you're serving this as a soup, accompany it with Strawberry Sorbet (page 182). On its own, it makes a perfect mixer, with a splash of tequila or gin.

MAKES 6 SERVINGS

Dessert Soups

43

Rhubarb Soup

Not only was this the most popular soup on my menu at Restaurant Daniel, but I received a bartender's certificate from *Bartender* magazine for creating it. It mixes nicely with vodka, but it was most famous there as part of a champagne cocktail: Just pour a half inch of the soup into the bottom of a champagne glass and fill the glass with champagne—magnificent! This soup is also a superb digestif. What gives it such flavor dimension is the grenadine and the lemongrass. If you can't find lemongrass, lemon zest makes an acceptable substitute. Serve with Citrus Sorbet (page 184).

MAKES 8 SERVINGS

Flavor Sachet

Grated zest of 1 lime

Grated zest of 1 orange

1 stalk lemongrass, chopped, or grated zest of 1 lemon

Soup

1 pound (about 7 medium stalks) (454 grams) rhubarb, trimmed, washed, and chopped

⅔ cup (134 grams) sugar

⅓ cup plus 1 tablespoon (100 grams) grenadine

Garnish

6 strawberries, washed and hulled

1 mango, peeled

2 passion fruit

8 mint sprigs

1. *Make the flavor sachet:* Place the lime zest, orange zest, and chopped lemongrass in the center of a 4-inch square of cheesecloth. Gather the corners of the square together to form a pouch and tie with a piece of kitchen string.

2. *Make the soup:* Combine the rhubarb, 4 cups (944 grams) water, and the sugar in a large saucepan and bring to a boil, stirring occasionally. Remove the pan from the heat; add the sachet and stir in the grenadine. Cover the pan and allow the flavors to infuse for 2 hours.

3. *Make the garnish:* Slice the strawberries lengthwise ⅛ inch thick. Stack the slices, a few at a time, on top of one another and cut the stacks into thin strips. Cut ⅛-inch-thick slices of mango flesh off the pit. Stack the slices, a few at a time, on top of one another and cut the stacks into thin strips (you will need 80 strips). Cut the passion fruit in half and scrape the seeds into a small container; reserve the fruit for another use.

4. *Serve the soup:* Divide the strawberry strips among eight soup bowls. Remove the sachet from the soup and whisk for a few seconds to break up the rhubarb fibers. Ladle the soup over the strawberry strips in each bowl. Arrange 10 mango strips in five crisscross patterns around the perimeter of each bowl. Spoon a few passion fruit seeds between the mango crisscrosses in each bowl. Garnish the soup with the mint sprigs.

Dessert
Soups

Rhubarb Soup

Blackberry-Pear Soup

Blackberry-Pear Soup

Soup

2 pints (454 grams) ripe blackberries

1 cup (200 grams) sugar

6 ripe Bartlett pears, peeled and cored

Garnish

6 mint sprigs

1. *Make the soup:* Combine the blackberries, sugar, and 2 cups (472 grams) water in a saucepan just large enough to hold the pears upright. Bring to a boil over medium-high heat, stirring to dissolve the sugar. Reduce the heat to medium-low and simmer for 3 minutes. Remove the pan from the heat and allow to cool for 10 minutes.

2. Transfer the berry mixture to a blender or food processor and process until smooth. Strain the purée through a fine-mesh sieve back into the saucepan. Trim the bottoms of the pears so they can stand upright. Add the pears to the berry mixture and bring to a boil over medium-high heat. Reduce the heat and simmer for 5 to 8 minutes, or until the pears are tender when pierced with a fork. (If the pears are not perfectly ripe, they will take longer to cook.) Remove the pan from the heat and cool completely.

3. Transfer the pears and soup to a large bowl, cover with plastic wrap, and refrigerate for at least 8 hours, or overnight.

4. *Serve the soup:* Place 1 pear upright in the center of each soup bowl. Pour the soup over the pears and garnish with the mint sprigs.

The best time for this soup is late summer/early autumn, when both of these fruits are in peak season. Blackberries that are not perfectly ripe will be too tart and will overwhelm the pear. I recommend Bartlett pears for flavor and juiciness when blackberries aren't in season. I have also made a pear soup with crème de cassis, a black currant liqueur. Serve with Citrus Sorbet (page 184).

MAKES 6 SERVINGS

Apple Soup

This fall soup could easily become part of your Thanksgiving tradition. I recommend McIntosh apples, because they are particularly flavorful and very juicy. But Idared and Granny Smith apples are fine second choices. Use a mandoline, if possible, to slice the apples; you want them as thin as can be. Serve with Citrus Sorbet (page 184).

MAKES 8 SERVINGS

Apple Chips

½ cup (57 grams) confectioners' sugar

1 McIntosh apple, cored and sliced crosswise into 1/16-inch rounds

Soup

8 (about 2½ pounds) (1 kilo) McIntosh apples, peeled, cored, and quartered

⅔ cup (134 grams) sugar

1 vanilla bean, split

Grated zest of 1 lemon

Garnish

1 McIntosh apple, cored, halved, and thinly sliced

1 teaspoon (5 grams) fresh lemon juice

8 mint sprigs

1. *Make the apple chips:* Preheat the oven to 275°F.

2. Sift half of the confectioners' sugar onto a nonstick baking sheet. Arrange the apple slices in a single layer on the baking sheet and sift the remaining confectioners' sugar over them. Bake the slices for 45 minutes. To check if they are done, remove one slice with a spatula and place it on a cool surface. If after 1 minute it hardens enough so that it will snap in half, the chips are ready. If it doesn't, continue to bake, checking at 15-minute intervals. When they are done, remove them from the pan and place them on a wire rack to cool. They can be stored in an airtight container in a cool dry place for up to 2 weeks.

3. *Make the soup:* Combine the apples, 4 cups (944 grams) water, the sugar, and vanilla bean in a medium saucepan and bring to a boil, stirring to dissolve the sugar. Reduce the heat to medium-low and simmer for 5 minutes, or until the apples can be pierced easily with a fork. Remove the pan from the heat and allow to cool for 10 minutes.

4. Carefully pour the soup into a food processor or blender in batches and process until smooth, 45 to 60 seconds. Strain the soup through a sieve into a medium bowl. Stir in the lemon zest and refrigerate the soup for at least 3 hours, or until thoroughly chilled.

5. *Make the garnish:* Stack a few of the apple slices on top of each other and cut them into thin strips. Toss the apple strips with the lemon juice. Repeat with the remaining apple slices.

6. *Serve the soup:* Divide the soup among eight shallow serving bowls and scatter the apple strips over the soup. Garnish each serving with an apple chip and a mint sprig.

Tropical Fruit Soup

Soup

⅔ cup (134 grams) sugar

Grated zest of 2 limes

Grated zest of 2 oranges

1 stalk lemongrass, chopped

1 tablespoon (15 grams) chopped ginger

1 vanilla bean, split

1 cinnamon stick

1 whole clove

2 tablespoons (12 grams) Chinese 5-spice powder

Garnish

1 papaya, peeled, halved, seeded, and thinly sliced

1 mango, peeled, pitted, and cut into thin strips

2 kiwi, peeled, quartered, and sliced

1 pineapple, peeled, quartered, cored, and thinly sliced

8 mint sprigs

*A*lthough this recipe calls for exotic fruits—mango, kiwi, pineapple, and papaya—the spiced "stock" is perfect for all winter fruits, in any combination that intrigues you. Garnish the soup with a scoop of Mango Sorbet (page 183).

MAKES 8 SERVINGS

1. *Make the soup:* Combine 4 cups (944 grams) water, the sugar, citrus zests, lemongrass, ginger, vanilla bean, and spices in a medium saucepan. Bring to a boil. Remove the pan from the heat and let stand for 15 minutes in order for the flavors to infuse. Strain the soup through a sieve into a medium bowl or large pitcher and refrigerate until well chilled, at least 3 hours.

2. *Serve the soup:* Arrange 5 papaya slices in a pinwheel pattern in each of eight shallow soup bowls. Place the mango strips and kiwi slices between the papaya slices. Arrange the pineapple slices in a ring around the other fruits. Pour the soup over the fruit and garnish with the mint sprigs.

Mango Soup with Gingered Raspberries

Mango Soup with Gingered Raspberries

Gingered Raspberries

2½ cups (500 grams) sugar

One ¾-inch piece (9 grams) ginger, sliced ⅛ inch thick

½ pint (250 grams) raspberries

Soup

1 stalk lemongrass, chopped

Grated zest of 1 orange

¼ vanilla bean, split

1 teaspoon (5 grams) peeled and chopped ginger

3 ripe mangoes, peeled, pitted, and cut into chunks

1½ cups (375 grams) unsweetened coconut milk

Juice of 2 limes

2 tablespoons (28 grams) good-quality light rum

Garnish

8 mint sprigs

1. *Make the gingered raspberries:* Combine ¾ cup (177 grams) water, the sugar, and ginger in a medium saucepan. Bring to a boil, stirring occasionally. Remove the pan from the heat and allow to cool to room temperature.

2. Place the raspberries in a medium bowl. Pour the cooled ginger syrup through a sieve onto the raspberries. Allow the raspberries to macerate while you prepare the soup.

3. *Make the soup:* Combine 1 cup (236 grams) water, the lemongrass, orange zest, vanilla bean, and ginger in a medium saucepan. Bring to a boil. Remove the pan from the heat and allow it to stand for 15 minutes in order for the flavors to infuse. Strain the soup through a sieve into a large glass measure with a spout.

4. Purée the mango chunks in a food processor or blender until smooth, about 1 minute. Pour in the strained soup base, add the coconut milk, lime juice, and rum, and process until combined.

5. *Serve the soup:* Divide the soup among eight shallow bowls. Spoon some of the gingered raspberries into each bowl and garnish with the mint sprigs.

I developed this soup at Lucas Carton in Paris, and sometimes we had a hard time getting it to the customers—all the cooks were drinking it in the kitchen! The soup embraces many tropical flavors: coconut, ginger, and mango, along with raspberries for their color and flavor. First you taste the mango, with a little coconut as a back-note, then comes a hint of the ginger. I also added a little white rum because the soup is, after all, inspired by the tropics; use a good-quality rum. Though dark, Myers's rum is a fine substitute. Serve with a scoop of Mango Sorbet (page 183).

MAKES 8 SERVINGS

*Dessert
Soups*

Winter Fruit Soup

*T*his is an ideal cold-weather dessert soup because that is when you have an abundance of citrus—oranges, limes, grapefruit. If you can find blood oranges, use their juice. Fresh fruit juice is the key element; using presqueezed or frozen juices will provide barely a shadow of the flavor of the soup made with fresh juices. Pomegranate seeds make a colorful and crunchy sweet-tart garnish for this soup (see Note). Serve this with Citrus Sorbet (page 184).

MAKES 8 SERVINGS

NOTE: Using a serrated knife, cut off the blossom end of the pomegranate, taking some of the white membranes but preserving the seeds. Score the skin lengthwise in four or five places. Immerse the fruit in a bowl of cold water for five minutes. With the fruit underwater, break it apart along the scored lines. Pull back the rind and allow the seeds to separate from the membranes: They will sink to the bottom of the bowl. Skim off the debris at the surface with a skimmer or sieve, then drain the seeds in a colander. Pat the seeds dry with a paper towel and store in the refrigerator, tightly covered, for up to two days.

Dessert
Soups

Soup

2 cups (484 grams) fresh orange juice (about 8 large oranges)

2 cups (484 grams) fresh pink grapefruit juice (about 2½ medium grapefruits)

1 cup (242 grams) fresh lime juice (about 6 limes)

2 tablespoons (30 grams) grenadine

1 ripe banana, peeled and cut into chunks

Garnish

2 limes

4 oranges

6 pink grapefruit

8 mint sprigs

Pomegranate seeds (optional)

1. *Make the soup:* Combine the orange juice, grapefruit juice, lime juice, grenadine, and banana in a food processor or blender and process until smooth. Strain the soup through a sieve into a medium bowl or large pitcher and refrigerate until thoroughly chilled, at least 3 hours.

2. *Make the garnish:* Remove the peel from the lime with a sharp vegetable peeler. With a paring knife, remove any bitter white pith from the strips of lime peel. Cut the peel into thin strips.

3. Half-fill a medium bowl with water and add 2 large handfuls of ice cubes; set aside. Half-fill a small saucepan with water and bring it to a boil. Add the lime zest and boil for 3 minutes, or until tender. Drain the zest and immediately plunge it into the ice water. Allow to cool in the ice water for 1 minute. With a slotted spoon, transfer the zest to a small container and refrigerate until ready to garnish the soup.

4. Using a paring knife, slice off the bottom and top of the oranges so that they stand upright. Slicing from top to bottom, cut away the peel, including the white part, in strips. Remove the orange segments, slicing between translucent membranes to release them. Repeat this process with the grapefruit. Refrigerate until ready to serve the soup.

5. *Serve the soup:* Arrange 3 orange segments alternated with 3 pink grapefruit segments in a pinwheel pattern in each of eight shallow soup bowls. Pour the soup over the fruit and garnish with the reserved lime zest strips, sprigs of mint, and pomegranate seeds, if desired.

Fricassee of Winter Fruits

1 orange

1 grapefruit

1 lime

1½ cups plus 1½ tablespoons (319 grams) sugar

2 pears

1 tablespoon (16 grams) fresh lemon juice

2 Granny Smith apples

4 tablespoons (57 grams) unsalted butter

12 cranberries

4 prunes

3 candied chestnuts, cut in half, optional
   (see Sources, page 225)

1 vanilla bean, split

2 tablespoons (28 grams) Armagnac, cognac, or Calvados

4 scoops Prune-Armagnac Ice Cream (page 177)

Let the produce section of your local market determine the exact contents of this fruit stew: The fruits called for here are just a suggested list, but they do work well together. No matter what winter fruits you choose, avoid the common mistake of sautéing them all at the same time, for the same amount of time. Firmer fruits like apple and pear take longer than citrus. Serve this with Prune-Armagnac Ice Cream (page 177); Caramel Ice Cream (page 179) or Vanilla Ice Cream (page 177) would be fine as well.

MAKES 4 SERVINGS

1. Using a serrated knife, slice off the bottom and top of the orange so that it stands upright: Slicing from top to bottom, cut away the peel, including the white part, in strips. Set the strips aside. Remove the orange segments, slicing between translucent membranes to release them. Repeat this process with the grapefruit, but do not reserve the grapefruit peel. Using a paring knife, slice off the bitter white part of the reserved orange strips.

2. Remove the zest from the lime with a sharp vegetable peeler. With the paring knife, remove any bitter white pith from the strips of lime zest. Cut the peel into thin strips.

3. Half-fill a medium saucepan with water and add the lime and orange zest. Bring to a boil. Drain the zest, and repeat the blanching process.

4. Combine 2 cups (472 grams) water and 1½ cups (300 grams) of the sugar in the saucepan and bring to a boil, stirring until the sugar is dissolved. Add the orange and lime zest and boil for 10 minutes. Allow to cool to room temperature.

5. Meanwhile, peel the pears. Using a melon baller, scoop out balls from the flesh. Toss the pear balls with the lemon juice in a medium bowl.

6. Peel and core the apples. Cut them in half and slice ¼ inch thick. Toss them with the pear balls and lemon juice.

continued

Dessert
Soups

54

Fricassee of Winter Fruits

7. Melt the butter in a large skillet over high heat. Add the apple slices and pear balls and sauté for 2 minutes until slightly softened. Drain the cooled orange and lime zest and add to the pan along with the remaining 1½ tablespoons (19 grams) sugar, the cranberries, prunes, and chestnuts, if using. Scrape the seeds from the vanilla bean into the pan and sauté for 2 minutes longer, until the sugar is dissolved. Add the orange and grapefruit segments and sauté for 2 minutes, until they are heated through. Add the Armagnac and cook for 1 minute longer, until the fruit absorbs its flavor. Spoon the fricassee into four shallow bowls and top each with a scoop of the ice cream.

Fricassee of Strawberries with Balsamic Vinegar

Although you are not using a lot of balsamic vinegar here, it is a crucial element to the success of this fricassee, so be sure to buy a quality one. But it doesn't have to be expensive; a good ten-year-old balsamic will do. The acidity of the vinegar opens your palate to the fruit, and what fruit is more amazing than peak-of-freshness strawberries? Serve with Vanilla Ice Cream (page 177).

MAKES 6 SERVINGS

1 tablespoon (14 grams) unsalted butter

2 tablespoons (25 grams) sugar

2 pints (452 grams) ripe strawberries, washed, hulled, and cut into quarters

1 tablespoon (15 grams) good-quality aged balsamic vinegar

1. Melt the butter in a large skillet over medium heat. Add the sugar and strawberries and cook, tossing the strawberries to coat them evenly, for about 1 minute. Add the balsamic vinegar and toss the strawberries until coated.

2. Spoon the strawberries into six shallow bowls and serve immediately.

Fricassee of Strawberries with Balsamic Vinegar

Cookies and Petits Fours

Of all the gifts America has given the world, I would have to rank the chocolate chip cookie somewhere near the top. The cookie recipes in this chapter are among the best cookies France has to offer. They include many of my favorites, both as boy and man: chewy Coconut Macaroons, crumbly Sablé Bretons, and whimsical Black-and-White Sugar Cookies. They are not all moist and chewy, which is the way Americans tend to prefer their cookies. Some will be familiar to you; others are sure to become part of your cookie repertoire. When it comes to cookies, you can never have too many recipes. Many of these doughs can be kept in the freezer, and you can remove just a portion of the dough and bake cookies as desired.

Petits fours are a part of my culinary heritage. French families often end a meal with petits fours, a little crunchy treat to accompany coffee or tea, or a serving of sorbet. In restaurants, petits fours are sometimes offered as a treat from the chef at the close to a meal. Although you may associate the term *petit four* with those small fondant-iced squares of cake, in France we use it to refer to a variety of small fancy cakes, tartlets, and cookies. The best petits fours have a distinctive but subtle flavor. The Pineapple Tea Cakes offer faint nutty notes to blend with pineapple. Apricot Tea Cakes are like fruitcakes, but with milder flavor and greater moisture. And the classic Financiers use an intriguing chewy texture to deliver the welcome flavor of almond.

Tuiles

7 tablespoons (100 grams) unsalted butter, softened

¾ cup plus 2 tablespoons (100 grams) confectioners' sugar

⅔ cup (97 grams) all-purpose flour

3 large egg whites

1. In an electric mixer fitted with the paddle attachment, beat the butter at medium speed until creamy, about 30 seconds. Add the confectioners' sugar and flour and mix until combined. Add the egg whites one at a time, beating after each addition just until well blended, about 1 minute in all. Refrigerate the batter for 30 minutes.

2. Preheat the oven to 350°F. Have a rolling pin at hand. Spray a baking sheet with nonstick cooking spray or line it with parchment paper.

3. Spoon 2 teaspoons of the batter onto the baking sheet and with a small, offset metal spatula, spread it evenly into a 3-inch circle. Repeat to form more tuiles, baking only 6 to 8 at a time. Refrigerate the remaining batter while you bake the tuiles.

4. Bake the tuiles for 4 to 6 minutes, until lightly browned around the edges. Remove from the oven and immediately shape the tuiles, lifting up each one with a metal spatula and draping it over the rolling pin so it curves, just until set. Repeat with the remaining batter. Store the tuiles in a cool dry place in an airtight container for up to 1 week.

A tuile is a crisp, thin cookie that adds a bit of sweetness and crunch to servings of ice cream, sorbet, mousse, and other creamy desserts. These plain tuiles are good, but tuiles are also commonly flavored with cocoa, orange, espresso, and other flavors. Recipes for Coconut Tuiles and Pistachio-Almond Tuiles follow this one. What is perhaps most noteworthy about tuiles is that they are pliable when just baked and still warm, so you can shape them into the traditional curved "roof tile" cookies, as in this recipe, or mold them into a variety of different shapes. For other ideas, see the suggestions on page 22.

MAKES ABOUT
25 TUILES

*Cookies
and
Petits
Fours*

Coconut Tuiles

Coconut Tuiles

2¼ cups (259 grams) confectioners' sugar

3⅓ cups (266 grams) unsweetened dried shredded coconut

2 tablespoons (28 grams) unsalted butter, melted

5 large eggs

1. Preheat the oven to 325°F. Spray a baking sheet with nonstick cooking spray, or use a nonstick sheet. Have a rolling pin at hand.

2. In the bowl of an electric mixer fitted with the paddle attachment, mix together the confectioners' sugar and coconut at low speed until combined. Add the melted butter and mix until combined. Add the eggs one at a time, mixing until each egg is incorporated before adding the next.

3. Spoon about 2 teaspoons of the tuile batter onto the baking sheet and, using the back of the spoon, spread it into a 3-inch round. Repeat until the baking sheet is full, leaving about 2 inches between the tuiles. Bake the tuiles for 10 to 12 minutes, until golden brown around the edges. Using a metal spatula, immediately remove one tuile from the sheet and drape it over the rolling pin, just until set. Repeat with the remaining tuiles. If the tuiles become difficult to remove from the sheet, return them to the oven for 30 seconds to make them more pliable. Cool the tuiles completely before removing from pan. Repeat with the remaining batter. Store the tuiles in an airtight container in a cool dry place for up to 1 week.

*A*lmond tuiles are very common, but you rarely see coconut tuiles. I don't understand why. This delicious cookie complements just about any sorbet or ice cream. The batter is dense, which makes it even easier to use it in the way tuiles are most commonly employed: as a decorative accent on a dessert. (See page 22 for suggestions on how to shape tuiles.)

MAKES ABOUT
28 TUILES

Cookies
and
Petits
Fours

Pistachio-Almond Tuiles

This cookie is the perfect, nut-crunchy accompaniment to ice cream or sorbet. It is very simple to make, and an easy recipe to adapt to other nuts. I know Americans love peanuts; if you decide to make a peanut tuile to pair with some chocolate ice cream, use unsalted peanuts. This dough is easy to spread on a nonstick baking sheet, but it is important that you let the pan cool between batches, or the cookies will stick to it. (Tuiles are fun to play with; see page 22.)

MAKES ABOUT 25 TUILES

⅓ cup (48 grams) all-purpose flour

¾ cup (86 grams) confectioners' sugar

Grated zest of ½ lemon

Grated zest of ½ orange

2 large egg whites, at room temperature

3 tablespoons (43 grams) unsalted butter, melted

3 tablespoons (28 grams) pistachio nuts, chopped

¼ cup (21 grams) sliced blanched almonds

1. In a mixer fitted with the paddle attachment, combine the flour, confectioners' sugar, lemon zest, and orange zest, and beat at low speed to mix. Add the egg whites and mix just until smooth, about 30 seconds; scrape down the side of the bowl with a rubber spatula as necessary. Add the melted butter and mix until blended. Cover the bowl with plastic wrap and refrigerate for 1 hour.

2. Preheat the oven to 350°F. Have a rolling pin at hand.

3. Spoon a small amount of batter onto a nonstick baking sheet and with the back of the spoon or your finger, spread it into a thin oval shape about 4 inches long and 1½ inches wide. Form 3 more ovals on the baking sheet. Sprinkle the batter lightly with a few of the pistachios and sliced almonds.

4. Bake the tuiles for 3 to 5 minutes, until light golden brown. Remove the sheet from the oven and, using a metal spatula, immediately drape each tuile over the rolling pin, pressing down gently on it so that it curves, just until set. Cool the tuiles completely on a wire rack. Repeat with the remaining batter. Store the tuiles in an airtight container in a cool dry place for up to 2 days.

Pistachio-Almond Tuiles

Coconut Macaroons

*W*e French love our maca- roons. We probably have as many different words for maca- roon as Eskimos are said to have for snow. This one is called *congolais* (meaning coconut petit four), though to you, it is just a maca- roon. This is a simple recipe that offers the full, intense flavor of co- conut in the classic sweet-nutty, crispy-on-the-outside-chewy-on- the-inside experience. Make sure to use unsweetened coconut (see page 7); the sweetened variety may be easier to find, but if you use it, the macaroons will be far too sweet.

MAKES ABOUT 38 MACAROONS

Special Equipment:
Pastry Bag Fitted with a ½-Inch Plain Tip (Such as Ateco #6)

9 large egg whites

1 cup (200 grams) sugar

4 cups plus 2 tablespoons (330 grams) unsweetened dried shredded coconut

1. Preheat the oven to 350°F. Spray a baking sheet with nonstick cooking spray.

2. In a large bowl, whisk together the egg whites, sugar, and coconut until well blended.

3. Fill a pastry bag fitted with a ½-inch plain tip. Pipe out 1-inch di- ameter balls onto the baking sheet, spacing them 1 inch apart. Moisten your fingertips in water and shape the balls into pyramids, pinching the batter with your fingertips.

4. Bake the macaroons for 26 to 28 minutes or until light golden brown. Cool the macaroons on the baking sheet for 10 minutes, then transfer them to a wire rack and cool completely. Store in an airtight con- tainer in a cool dry place for up to 3 days.

Black-and-White Sugar Cookies

½ pound plus 1 tablespoon (2 sticks plus 1 tablespoon) (241 grams) unsalted butter, softened

2¾ cups (400 grams) all-purpose flour

1⅓ cups (153 grams) confectioners' sugar

1 large egg

1 tablespoon (12 grams) pure vanilla extract

Grated zest of 1 lemon

2 tablespoons (12 grams) unsweetened alkalized cocoa powder

1 large egg white, beaten

1. In an electric mixer fitted with the paddle attachment, beat the butter with the flour and confectioners' sugar on low speed until the mixture is crumbly, about 30 seconds. Add the egg, vanilla extract, and lemon zest and mix just until combined. Remove about one third of the dough to a lightly floured work surface and divide it into four pieces. Roll each piece under the palms of your hands into a 9-inch log that is about ½ inch in diameter. Place the logs on a baking sheet and freeze while you make the chocolate dough.

2. Add the cocoa powder to the dough remaining in the bowl and mix on low speed just until combined, about 30 seconds. Place the chocolate dough on the lightly floured work surface and divide it into three pieces, making one of them slightly larger than the other two. Divide each of the smaller pieces in half and roll each of these pieces into a 9-inch-long log. Place the logs on the baking sheet with the other logs in the freezer.

3. Divide the remaining piece of chocolate dough in half. Roll one of the pieces between two sheets of wax paper into a 8½ × 5-inch rectangle. Repeat with the other piece of dough. Remove the top sheet of waxed paper from each rectangle. Place the dough rectangles on a baking sheet and refrigerate for 30 minutes.

4. Remove the logs from the freezer. Place a plain and a chocolate log next to each other on a baking sheet. With a pastry brush, brush the top of the logs with the beaten egg white. Place a second layer of logs on top, with the plain log on top of the chocolate one, and vice versa. Press the logs gently together. Make a second separate stack with the remaining logs. Trim the ends of the dough stacks to even them.

continued

These black-and-white checkerboard cookies are enormously popular in my shop, and they are not as difficult to make as they look. The recipe is a classic French sugar cookie. The dough is divided, and cocoa is added to the larger portion. Logs of the two doughs are stacked so that the colors contrast, and then the logs are wrapped in cocoa dough. The sculpted dough can be kept in the freezer for several weeks and portions removed, as needed. If you like, you can top the cookies with a generous sprinkle of granulated sugar, which will crystallize in the oven and add a sweet crunch.

MAKES ABOUT 40 COOKIES

Cookies and Petits Fours

5. Remove the dough rectangles from the refrigerator. Brush the dough lightly with the egg white. Wrap one rectangle of chocolate dough around one stack of dough logs, overlapping the dough slightly at the seam and removing the wax paper as you wrap. Gently press the seam together to seal it. Repeat with the remaining dough rectangle and stack. Wrap the logs in plastic wrap and chill for 20 minutes or up to 3 days.

6. Preheat the oven to 350°F. Spray a large baking sheet with non-stick cooking spray or line it with parchment paper.

7. Unwrap the dough, slice it into ¼-inch slices, and arrange the cookies on the prepared baking sheet, allowing 1 inch between them. Bake the cookies for 16 to 18 minutes, until set; they should not color. Transfer the cookies to a wire rack to cool. Store the cookies in an airtight container in a cool dry place for up to 2 weeks.

Black-and-White Sugar Cookies   67

Apricot Tea Cakes

Apricot Tea Cakes

⅔ cup (189 grams) almond paste

2 large eggs

13 (about one and a quarter 15½-ounce cans) canned apricot halves in syrup, drained

3 tablespoons (27 grams) all-purpose flour

Pinch of salt

4 tablespoons (57 grams) unsalted butter, melted

1. Combine the almond paste, eggs, and 8 of the apricot halves in a food processor and process until smooth, about 20 seconds. Add the flour and salt and process until blended. Add the melted butter and process for 1 minute. Pour the batter into a liquid glass measure with a spout. Chill the batter for 20 minutes.

2. Preheat the oven to 350°F. Line 36 mini-muffin cups with paper petit four cups.

3. Slice the remaining 5 apricot halves lengthwise into ¼-inch strips. Pour the batter into the paper muffin cups, filling them to ⅛ inch from the tops. Arrange an apricot slice on top of each.

4. Bake the cakes for 30 to 35 minutes, until they are golden and a toothpick inserted in the center comes out clean. Let cool in the pan on a wire rack. Repeat with the remaining batter. Store in an airtight container at room temperature for up to a week.

*T*hese mini-cakes are great for any holiday, but particularly for Christmas. They're like baby-size fruitcakes, but very moist and delicious. People love them; trays of these are sold in my shop every day. During the winter, when the air is very dry, I brush these with Apricot Glaze (page 33) to keep them moist. In summer, with the humidity, it is not as important. This recipe can also be made with pears or pineapple.

**MAKES ABOUT
36 PETITS FOURS**

Special Equipment:
Two Mini-Muffin Pans (1-Ounce Cups); Thirty-Six 1-Inch Paper Petit Four Cups

Galette Noisette

This is similar to the Sablé Bretons (page 75), but because there is no baking powder, it is a denser cookie. Rich and buttery, it carries the distinct flavor of hazelnut from the hazelnut flour, which is in fact finely ground hazelnuts. In France, both of these cookies are an after-school treat for kids. Try them on the kids, but reserve some for yourself for the coffee hour.

MAKES ABOUT 30 COOKIES

Special Equipment:
2-Inch Round Cookie Cutter

½ pound plus 1 tablespoon (2 sticks plus 1 tablespoon) (240 grams) unsalted butter, softened

1 cup plus 2 tablespoons (100 grams) hazelnut flour (see Sources, page 225)

¾ cup (97 grams) cake flour

½ cup (100 grams) sugar

Pinch of salt

1 large egg yolk

1. In an electric mixer fitted with the paddle attachment, beat the butter, hazelnut flour, cake flour, sugar, and salt at low speed until combined. Add the egg yolk and mix at medium speed until combined. Shape the dough into a disc and wrap it well in plastic wrap. Refrigerate for at least 2 hours.

2. Preheat the oven to 325°F. Grease a large baking sheet or line it with parchment paper.

3. Divide the dough in half. On a lightly floured work surface, roll the dough out to a thickness of ¼ inch. Using a 2-inch round cookie cutter, cut out cookies and place 1 inch apart on the prepared baking sheet. Reroll the scraps and cut out more cookies.

4. Bake the cookies for 8 to 10 minutes, until golden brown. Cool the cookies on a wire rack. Repeat with the remaining dough. Store in an airtight container in a cool dry place for up to 2 weeks.

Galette Noisette

Pistachio-Almond Biscotti

Pistachio-Almond Biscotti

3 tablespoons (43 grams) unsalted butter, softened

½ cup plus 2 tablespoons (125 grams) sugar

1½ cups plus 2 tablespoons (235 grams) all-purpose flour

1 teaspoon (5 grams) baking powder

Pinch of salt

Grated zest of 1 lemon

2 large eggs

⅔ cup (80 grams) slivered almonds

⅓ cup (50 grams) shelled pistachio nuts

1 tablespoon (6 grams) anise seeds

*T*his twice-baked Italian cookie is classically crumbly and crunchy, and they strike some people (like me) as extremely dry. But that's intentional—they are designed to be dipped in coffee (or milk); some people enjoy them dipped in wine.

MAKES ABOUT
30 BISCOTTI

1. Preheat the oven to 350°F. Line a baking sheet with parchment or wax paper.

2. In the bowl of an electric mixer fitted with the paddle attachment, beat the butter and sugar on medium speed until combined, about 1 minute. Add the flour, baking powder, salt, and lemon zest and beat just until combined. Add the eggs one at a time, beating well after each addition and scraping down the side of the bowl as necessary. Add the nuts and anise seeds and mix until combined.

3. Transfer the dough to a lightly floured work surface and shape it into a 12-inch-long log. Transfer the log to the prepared baking sheet with a spatula. Bake for 30 minutes, or until the top is firm to the touch. Allow the log to cool on the baking sheet for 10 minutes. Leave the oven on.

4. Using a sharp serrated knife, cut the log on the diagonal into ½-inch-thick slices. Place the biscotti cut side up on the lined baking sheet and bake for an additional 12 to 14 minutes, or until golden brown and crisp. Cool completely on a wire rack. Store the biscotti in an airtight container in a cool dry place for up to 2 weeks.

Financiers

This is the quintessential, traditional French petit four. These little cakes have a slightly crunchy exterior and a buttery-nutty flavor; the inside is tender, the outside a bit chewy. Don't be concerned when they start to crack and dome as they bake; that is the traditional look. The financier is a great accompaniment for ice creams and sorbets.

**MAKES ABOUT
20 PETITS FOURS**

Special Equipment:
Two Mini-Muffin Pans (1-Ounce Cups); Twenty 1-Inch Paper Petit Four Cups

½ cup (60 grams) slivered almonds

¼ cup (29 grams) confectioners' sugar

¼ cup (32 grams) cake flour

¼ cup (50 grams) granulated sugar

3 large egg whites

4 tablespoons (57 grams) unsalted butter, melted and still hot

1. Preheat the oven to 350°F. Line 20 mini-muffin cups with paper petit four cups or oval paper cups.

2. Place the slivered almonds in a food processor and process until finely ground, but do not overprocess. Transfer to the bowl of an electric mixer.

3. Sift the confectioners' sugar and cake flour over the almonds. Add the granulated sugar and, using the whisk attachment, mix on low speed until combined. Add the egg whites one at a time, beating well after each addition. Scrape down the side of the bowl with a rubber spatula. With the mixer on, add the hot melted butter in a thin stream and mix until blended, about 30 seconds. Transfer the batter to a glass measure with a spout.

4. Pour the batter into the paper cups, filling them three-quarters full. Bake the financiers for 20 to 25 minutes, until golden and a toothpick inserted in the center of a cake comes out clean. Cool completely in the pan on a wire rack. Store in an airtight container for up to a week.

Sablé Bretons

2⅓ cups (303 grams) cake flour

1 tablespoon plus 1 teaspoon (20 grams) baking powder

1¼ teaspoons (8 grams) salt

4 large egg yolks

1 cup (200 grams) sugar

½ pound (2 sticks) (227 grams) unsalted butter, softened

1 tablespoon (5 grams) instant coffee granules

1 egg, lightly beaten

1. Sift together the flour, baking powder, and salt into a medium bowl. Gently whisk together until well blended.

2. In an electric mixer fitted with the whisk attachment, beat the egg yolks and sugar at medium speed until combined, about 1 minute. Beat in the butter just until combined. Add the dry ingredients and mix at low speed until blended, scraping down the side of the bowl with a rubber spatula once or twice. Cover the bowl with plastic wrap and refrigerate the dough for at least 2 hours.

3. Preheat the oven to 350°F. Line a large baking sheet with parchment or wax paper.

4. On a lightly floured work surface, pat the the dough into a rough circle. Roll it out with a rolling pin to a thickness of ¼ inch. Using a 2-inch round cookie cutter, cut out the cookies and place them ¾ inch apart on the prepared baking sheet. Continue rerolling the scraps and cutting out more cookies until all the dough is used.

5. In a small bowl, whisk the instant coffee and 2 tablespoons (30 grams) boiling water together until the coffee is dissolved. Whisk in the egg. Lightly brush the cookies with the egg mixture. Let stand for 10 minutes. Brush the cookies again with the egg mixture.

6. Bake the cookies for 18 to 20 minutes, until the edges are just golden brown. Cool the cookies on a wire rack. Store in an airtight container in cool dry place for up to 2 weeks.

Sablé—the word translates as "sand"—cookies have a pleasantly dry and crumbly texture. This version is from Brittany; Bretons are famous for liking their salt (some of the best sea salt in the world comes from the Breton coast), and the dough has a characteristic touch of salt. This sablé has a buttery flavor that I can only describe as being "very French." It is one of my favorite cookies to eat with ice cream or sorbet; it goes with any flavor you can name. It is very rich, so two cookies are enough with sorbet.

**MAKES ABOUT
50 COOKIES**

Special Equipment:
2-Inch Round Cookie Cutter

*Cookies
and
Petits
Fours*

Pineapple Tea Cakes

Pineapple Tea Cakes

1 pound, 10 ounces (750 grams) almond paste

2 tablespoons (35 grams) apricot preserves

5 large eggs

3 large egg yolks

½ cup plus 1 tablespoon (81 grams) all-purpose flour

14 tablespoons (1¾ sticks) (200 grams) unsalted butter, melted

1 pineapple, peeled, quartered, cored, and cut into ¼-inch cubes

Garnish

2 tablespoons (14 grams) confectioners' sugar

1. Preheat the oven to 350°F. Arrange one hundred 1-inch paper petit four cups on a large baking sheet.

2. In an electric mixer fitted with the paddle attachment, combine the almond paste and apricot preserves and beat at medium speed until smooth. Beat in the eggs one a time, mixing until each egg is incorporated before adding the next. Beat in the egg yolks one at a time. Beat in the flour at low speed. Add the melted butter and mix until blended.

3. Fill a pastry bag fitted with a ¼-inch plain tip with the batter. Pipe the batter into the paper cups, filling them three-quarters full. Place a cube of pineapple on top of each cup. Sift the confectioners' sugar over the cups.

4. Bake the cakes for 25 to 28 minutes, or until light golden brown. Let cool on the baking sheet. Store in an airtight container at room temperature for up to a week.

*T*his is a refreshing and elegant petit four. The cake has a slight nutty note to contrast with the sweet fruit, and the miniature paper baking cups give it its distinctive fluted appearance. Each small cake is garnished with a piece of pineapple, but I've also made raisin tea cakes with raisins soaked in rum instead of the pineapple. The almond paste and apricot preserves add both flavor and moisture. Be sure to use almond paste, not marzipan, which is made from more or less the same ingredients but, unlike the paste, is cooked. You could replace the preserves with apricot marmalade. These will keep in a tin for at least a week.

**MAKES ABOUT
100 PETITS FOURS**

Special Equipment:
One Hundred 1-Inch Paper Petit Four Cups; Pastry Bag Fitted with a ¼-Inch Plain Tip (Such as Ateco #2)

*Cookies
and
Petits
Fours*

Weekend Cakes

A weekend cake is one that does not have to be refrigerated. It is designed to travel: Just throw it in a bag and go. It is perfect for a picnic: It can sit out for hours and still retain its texture and flavor. It is designed to keep: Leave it on the kitchen counter for your family, weekend guests, or drop-in visitors to cut a slice and enjoy. A weekend cake is a no-headache cake. My mother made one of these every week and just left it out for us to take some after school.

These easy cakes depend on the addition of dry ingredients like nuts and coconuts and dried fruit for their flavor. Several of them also contain alcohol—dark rum—but in such a small amount that it only brings a hint of flavor to the cake; it is a backnote, not distinct at all.

Well wrapped in plastic, these cakes will keep at room temperature for three or four days. For longer storage, they can be kept in the refrigerator for up to a week.

Golden Banana Cake

1 cup (145 grams) all-purpose flour

⅛ teaspoon baking powder

Pinch of baking soda

8 tablespoons (1 stick) (113 grams) unsalted butter, softened

1½ tablespoons (20 grams) olive oil

¾ cup (150 grams) sugar

4 large eggs

1 extra-ripe medium banana, peeled and mashed

One day I wanted to use up a case of bananas that were overripe, and this cake was the result. The olive oil adds moisture to the cake. You can serve this cake warm; it is very rewarding with Vanilla Ice Cream (page 177).

MAKES 8 SERVINGS

1. Preheat the oven to 325°F. Butter an 8½ × 4½ × 2½-inch loaf pan. Dust the pan with flour, tapping out the excess.

2. Sift together the flour, baking powder, and baking soda.

3. In the bowl of an electric mixer fitted with the paddle attachment, mix together the butter, olive oil, and sugar at low speed. Increase the speed to medium and add the eggs one at a time, beating well after each addition. Mix in the mashed banana. Add the flour mixture and mix just until combined. Scrape the batter into the prepared pan, smoothing the top with a spatula.

4. Bake the cake for 55 to 60 minutes, until the top is golden brown and a toothpick inserted in the center of the cake comes out clean. Cool the cake in the pan on a wire rack for 15 minutes. Unmold the cake and cool completely on the rack. Store in an airtight container at room temperature for 3 days, 1 week refrigerated, or 2 months frozen.

Lemon Pound Cake

Lemon Pound Cake

1 cup plus 2 tablespoons (146 grams) cake flour

⅛ teaspoon baking powder

3 large eggs

1 cup (200 grams) sugar

⅛ teaspoon salt

Grated zest of 1½ lemons

¼ cup plus 2 tablespoons (87 grams) heavy cream

6 tablespoons (86 grams) unsalted butter, melted and cooled

1. Preheat the oven to 325°F. Butter an 8½ × 4½ × 2½-inch loaf pan. Dust the pan with flour, tapping out the excess.

2. Sift together the flour and baking powder.

3. In an electric mixer fitted with the whisk attachment, beat the eggs at medium speed until blended. Gradually add the sugar and salt and beat until thickened and pale, about 2 minutes. At low speed, mix in the dry ingredients and lemon zest alternately with the heavy cream. Add the melted butter and mix until combined. Scrape the batter into the prepared pan, smoothing the top with a spatula.

4. Bake for 1 hour and 5 to 10 minutes, until the top of the cake is golden and a toothpick inserted in the center comes out clean. Cool the cake in the pan on a rack for 15 minutes. Remove the cake from the pan and cool completely on the rack.

This is my father's recipe. He would make a big batch of the batter and keep it in the freezer, then take out some of it every Wednesday and bake it up. On Wednesdays, we didn't have school; I would stay home and do homework or go out to play, knowing that the lemon pound cake would be there at day's end.

The batter is not heavy, but it bakes into a dense cake. The more airy a cake, the faster it dries; the more dense, the longer it retains its moisture. You can make as many of these cakes as you like, wrap them well in plastic, and freeze them. The night before you intend to serve it, take one out and put it in the refrigerator to thaw. This is great for breakfast, sliced and warmed up in the toaster, as well as perfect at afternoon tea.

MAKES 10 TO 12 SERVINGS

Apple Cake

My father created this recipe twenty years ago, and he still sells one hundred of these apple cakes a day from his shop in Nice. The only time he changes the formula is when his preferred apple—*la reine des reinettes*—is not available. Then, because his customers demand some kind of cake, he makes it with apricot. As always, I follow my father's lead. First, when selecting an apple for this cake, find one that is nice and plump. A Rome apple or a Fuji will, like my father's favorite, retain moisture no matter how long it is baked. Second, if you like the idea of this recipe with apricots rather than apples, please try it. (Substitute fifteen to twenty apricot halves for the apples.) When it is baked, an apricot has such wonderful acidity. In fact, I like that even better, but I know that Americans love apples. This will keep in the refrigerator for a week. (The apricot version will last for only two days or so.) This is best served plain.

MAKES 10 TO 12 SERVINGS

⅓ cup (60 grams) raisins

3 tablespoons (42 grams) dark rum, such as Myers's

1 scant cup (136 grams) all-purpose flour

¾ teaspoon (3 grams) baking powder

8 tablespoons (1 stick) (113 grams) unsalted butter, softened

1 cup (115 grams) confectioners' sugar

3 large eggs

2 apples, such as Fuji or Rome, peeled and cored

¼ cup (60 grams) Apricot Glaze (page 33)

1. Preheat the oven to 325°F. Butter an 8½ × 4½ × 2½-inch loaf pan. Dust the pan with flour, tapping out the excess.

2. Bring a small pan of water to a boil, add the raisins, and boil 1 minute. Drain and repeat the process. Drain the raisins well a second time and place in a small bowl with the rum; stir and set aside.

3. Sift together the flour and baking powder.

4. In the bowl of an electric mixer fitted with the paddle attachment, mix together the butter and confectioners' sugar on medium speed. Add the eggs one at a time, beating well after each addition. Scrape down the side of the bowl with a rubber spatula. Mix in the raisins and rum. Add the dry ingredients and mix on low speed until blended. Spoon half of the batter into the pan and smooth into an even layer.

5. Cut one apple into 12 wedges and arrange them over the batter, down the center of the pan, so their sides touch and the domed side of each wedge is on top. Spoon the rest of the batter over and around the apples and smooth the top. Cut the other apple into 8 wedges and then cut each wedge in half crosswise. Arrange the wedges in a single row along each long side of the pan, pressing the center-cut sides of the apples against the sides of the pan. There will be two rows of apple slices, with their points toward the center of the pan and exposed batter in the center. Gently push the apples into the batter, leaving the top of the apples exposed.

6. Bake the cake for 60 to 65 minutes, until the top is golden brown and a toothpick inserted in the center comes out clean. Cool the cake in the pan on a wire rack for 15 minutes. Unmold the cake and turn it right side up. Gently brush the apricot glaze over the top of the hot cake. Allow the cake to cool completely before cutting into slices.

Apple Cake

Gâteau Basque

This is a slight reworking of a traditional French cake. It has the feel and flavor of the old-fashioned French bistros, which have become so popular in America. Philippe Bertineau, the executive chef at Payard, gave me this recipe and encouraged me to sell it in the shop, and it has done very well. It is very moist because there is pastry cream in the batter, and the touch of almonds gives it sublime flavor. The classic Gâteau Basque contains raisins, but Philippe prefers cherries, either black or sour cherries. Don't be afraid of sour cherries; the slight acidity they bring ties these flavors together. You can eliminate the rum, if you like, or you can substitute orange flower water. This makes two cakes, but they keep well. This cake will keep in the refrigerator for a week, or in the freezer for a month.

**MAKES TWO 8-INCH
ROUND CAKES**
(8 to 10 Servings Each)

Special Equipment:
Pastry Bag Fitted with a ½-Inch
Plain Tip (Such as Ateco #6)

*Weekend
Cakes*

¾ cup (90 grams) slivered almonds

1⅓ cups (193 grams) all-purpose flour

1 teaspoon (5 grams) baking powder

4 large eggs

1 cup (200 grams) sugar

1 vanilla bean, split

14 tablespoons (1¾ sticks) (200 grams) unsalted butter, melted and cooled

1 tablespoon (14 grams) dark rum, such as Myers's

1⅓ cups (333 grams) Pastry Cream (page 28), at room temperature

10 ounces (283 grams) black or sour cherries, pitted

1. Place the almonds in the bowl of a food processor and process until finely ground, about 45 seconds. Transfer to a medium bowl.

2. Sift the flour and baking powder over the almonds. Gently whisk until combined and set aside.

3. Place 3 eggs and the sugar in a large bowl. Scrape the seeds from the vanilla bean into the bowl (reserve the pod for another use) and whisk the eggs until thickened and pale. Whisk in the melted butter. Whisk in the dry ingredients and rum. Let the batter stand for 20 minutes.

4. Preheat the oven to 400°F. Butter two 8-inch round cake pans. Dust the pans with flour, tapping out the excess.

5. Put the pastry cream into a medium bowl and whisk it until smooth. Fill a pastry bag fitted with a ½-inch plain tip with the pastry cream. Scrape ¾ cup of the cake batter into each cake pan and smooth the top with a spatula. Pipe the pastry cream over the batter in each pan, beginning ¼ inch from the edge of the pan and piping in a loose spiral toward the center, leaving about 1 inch between the coils. Arrange the cherries over the pastry cream, dividing them evenly between the two cakes. Scrape the remaining cake batter over the cherries, dividing it evenly, and smooth it into an even layer, covering the cherries as much as possible. Lightly beat the remaining egg and lightly brush the tops of the cakes with the egg wash.

6. Bake the cakes for 30 to 35 minutes, until golden brown on top and a toothpick inserted into the center comes out clean. Cool the cakes in the pans on a rack for 10 minutes. Invert the cakes onto the rack and cool completely; reinvert the cakes to serve.

Fruitcake

⅓ cup (60 grams) raisins

3 tablespoons (42 grams) dark rum, such as Myers's

1 cup (145 grams) all-purpose flour

1 teaspoon (5 grams) baking powder

2 large eggs, separated

7 tablespoons (100 grams) unsalted butter, softened

¾ cup (86 grams) confectioners' sugar

½ cup (80 grams) candied fruit, rinsed, drained, and cut into small dice

1. Place the raisins and rum in a small airtight container and allow to soak for at least 8 hours, or overnight.

2. Preheat the oven to 325°F. Butter an 8½ × 4½ × 2½-inch loaf pan. Dust the pan with flour, tapping out the excess.

3. Sift together the flour and baking powder.

4. In the clean dry bowl of an electric mixer fitted with the whisk attachment, beat the egg whites on low speed until frothy. Gradually increase the speed to high and beat until stiff peaks form.

5. In another mixer bowl, with the paddle attachment, mix the butter and sugar at low speed until blended. Increase the speed to medium and add the egg yolks one at a time, blending well after each addition. Mix in the candied fruit. Drain the raisins and mix them in. Remove the bowl from the mixer stand and, using a large rubber spatula, gently fold in the dry ingredients in two additions, alternating them with the beaten egg whites in two additions. Scrape the batter into the prepared pan and smooth the top with a spatula.

6. Bake the cake for 40 to 45 minutes, until the top is golden brown and a toothpick inserted in the center comes out clean. Cool the cake in the pan on a rack for 10 minutes. Unmold the cake and turn it right side up. Cool completely before serving.

I wish every American could try a freshly made fruitcake from a pâtisserie in France. Then, perhaps, they would understand why this cake is such an important tradition with us. But I'm not on a crusade. Mindful that Americans have a different palate, I've changed the traditional recipe a little bit. The classic French fruitcake is drenched in sherry. I use dark rum, and less of it. It is sweet enough and, for me, has more character. I've added some baking powder, just for a little rise, to make the cake a little puffy and not so heavy. A fruitcake must be studded with dried fruits, but it is completely up to you which fruits you use. You can use cherries, orange or lemon candy peels, or even just raisins. Dried grapefruit works very well too. This cake is perfect with a cup of coffee. It will keep for a week or more in the refrigerator.

MAKES 10 TO 12 SERVINGS

Weekend Cakes

Pain d'Épices

*P*ain d'épices is a traditional French spice cake. It can be sliced and toasted for breakfast, or used in a dessert, or even for cooking. At Payard, chef Philippe Bertineau cuts our pain d'épices into very thin slices, brushes them with clarified butter, crisps them under the broiler, and serves them with a shrimp dish. Even though there are many spices in the recipe, it is the honey that makes the difference. I strongly recommend pine honey. Pastis is a licorice-flavored French apéritif; it's optional, but I like the hint of licorice it adds.

This cake tastes best two or three days after it is made. The spices work with the honey and the wonderful flavor matures. Let it cool and put it in the refrigerator; it will keep for a week. Serve it like a pound cake with spiced pears and Caramel Ice Cream (page 179) for something truly memorable.

MAKES 4 LOAVES

Special Equipment:
Four 5¾ × 3¼ × 2-Inch Aluminum Foil Baby Loaf Pans

Weekend
Cakes

1 cup (336 grams) honey

¾ cup (150 grams) sugar

2 tablespoons (28 grams) dark rum, such as Myers's

2 pieces star anise

2 cups (170 grams) nuts, preferably a mix of sliced and slivered almonds, skinned pistachios, blanched hazelnuts, walnut halves, and pine nuts

1 cup (150 grams) diced dried fruit (¼-inch dice), preferably ¼ cup each apricots, figs, prunes, and dates

¼ cup (45 grams) dark raisins

¼ cup (45 grams) golden raisins

Grated zest of 1 lemon

Grated zest of 1 orange

1 tablespoon plus 1 teaspoon (20 grams) baking soda

1 teaspoon (5 grams) pastis, optional

¼ teaspoon ground cinnamon

¼ teaspoon (1 gram) freshly grated nutmeg

¼ teaspoon (1 gram) ground cloves, optional

Pinch of salt

3 cups (435 grams) all-purpose flour, sifted

1. Preheat the oven to 350°F. Butter four 5¾ × 3¼ × 2-inch aluminum foil or metal baby loaf pans. Dust the pans with flour and tap out the excess. Place the pans on a baking sheet.

2. Combine 1¾ cups (413 grams) water, the honey, sugar, rum, and star anise in a medium saucepan and bring to a boil. Meanwhile, combine the remaining ingredients except the flour in a large bowl.

3. Remove and discard the star anise and pour the liquid over the fruit and nut mixture. Let stand, stirring gently every now and then, for 5 minutes, then stir in the flour. Let the mixture stand for 2 to 3 minutes.

4. Divide the batter evenly among the pans, filling them about three-quarters full. Slide the baking sheet into the oven and bake for 45 to 50 minutes, or until a knife inserted into the center of the cakes comes out with a few moist crumbs clinging to the tip. Transfer the cakes to a rack to cool completely.

5. Unmold the cakes and wrap in plastic wrap. You can cut the cakes into thin slices when cool, but it's better to let them ripen for 3 days at room temperature. The cakes can also be wrapped airtight and frozen for up to a month.

Pain d'Epices

Chocolate Cakes

Everyone dreams of making a great chocolate cake at home, and as far as I'm concerned, it is a noble dream. Chocolate cakes not only are delicious, but they seem to strike a chord with people, having to do with home, comfort, celebrations, and good times.

Professional pastry chefs are not immune to this cake fixation, and there is a tradition of competing to make the largest and most elaborate cakes. I've read about cakes with thirty and more tiers, and elaborate sculptural and architectural decorative touches in sugar and fondant and gum paste, some of which even moved. Pastry chefs today still regard cake making as an essential discipline and a matter of pride, but happily, we concentrate our skills on more important details: flavor, balance, and precision. When I teach pastry classes, I spend time on pointing out the importance of sharp, clean edges and cuts, of uniform layers, and of artful icing. These are all skills that are within reach of the home cook.

The twelve chocolate cakes in this chapter are delicious and easy to do, and they require only a minimum of kitchen time. You will find an extremely dense chocolate cake (Chocolate Pudding Cake), a light cake with an oozing chocolate center (Chocolate Soufflé Cake), a brownie-like cake packed with moist pears (Chocolate-Pear Cake), and a silky smooth mousse cake (Milk-and-Dark-Chocolate Mousse Cake). Our cakes range in presentation from Old World elegant (Chocolate Charlotte) to 1990s sleek (Chocolate Mikado Cake) to the whimsical (Hedgehog Cake). If you like, you can use some of the decorating touches starting on page 18 to make them even more special.

Chocolate Soufflé Cake

6 ounces (170 grams) extra-bittersweet or bittersweet chocolate, chopped

10 tablespoons (1¼ sticks) (142 grams) unsalted butter, cut into tablespoons

3 large eggs, separated

1½ teaspoons (4 grams) all-purpose flour

7 tablespoons (86 grams) sugar

1 large egg white

1 teaspoon (3 grams) cream of tartar

8 scoops Pistachio (page 181) or Vanilla Ice Cream (page 177), optional

1. Generously grease eight 4-ounce disposable aluminum cups or ramekins with butter. Chill the ramekins in the freezer for 15 minutes.

2. Preheat the oven to 375°F. Brush the ramekins again with butter and coat them with sugar, tapping out the excess. Place the ramekins in a large roasting pan.

3. Fill a large saucepan one-third full with water and bring to a simmer. Place the chocolate and butter in a bowl, set over the simmering water, and heat, stirring frequently, until the chocolate is melted and the mixture is smooth. Set the chocolate mixture aside to cool.

4. In the bowl of an electric mixer fitted with the whisk attachment, beat the egg yolks at medium speed until blended. Beat in the flour, then beat in 5 tablespoons (63 grams) of the sugar, 1 tablespoon at a time. Increase the speed to high and beat the mixture until thickened and pale, about 3 minutes. Remove the bowl from the mixer stand and whisk in the cooled chocolate mixture.

5. In a clean dry mixer bowl, with the cleaned whisk attachment, beat the 4 egg whites on low speed until foamy. Add the cream of tartar and beat on medium speed until soft peaks form. Gradually beat in the remaining 2 tablespoons (25 grams) sugar. Increase the speed to high and beat until stiff peaks form. Using a rubber spatula, fold a scoop of the beaten whites into the chocolate mixture. Gently fold in the remaining whites.

6. Fill a large pastry bag fitted with a ½-inch plain tip with the soufflé mixture. Pipe the mixture into the ramekins, filling them three-quarters full. Pour enough hot water into the roasting pan to come halfway up the sides of the ramekins.

7. Bake the soufflés for 25 to 30 minutes, until the tops are cracked and puffed; a toothpick inserted into the center of a cake should come out moist and the center should be runny. Invert the soufflés onto dessert plates and serve immediately, with ice cream, if desired.

I put this cake on the menu as a special at Le Bernardin when I first came to America. Initially, there was resistance from management and kitchen staff, because the recipe takes liberties with classic elements of pastry. A cake with a runny center? A soufflé but not a soufflé? At the time, no one was doing anything like this, but my philosophy has always been that I'm not there to make just what I want on the menu; I also want to make what my customers want. And they want chocolate flavor, and fun. This cake turned out to be so popular it has been on the menu at Le Bernardin for nine years. It is a simple, rich, pure chocolate experience. And remember, it should be runny in the center. You can garnish it with a chocolate decoration (see page 18) and serve with pistachio or vanilla ice cream.

MAKES 8 SERVINGS

Special Equipment:
Eight 4-Ounce Ramekins;
Pastry Bag Fitted with a ½-Inch
Plain Tip (Such as Ateco #6)

Chocolate Cakes

Chocolate Pudding Cake

Pudding is a somewhat deceptive term here. This cake is more like a giant serving of ganache. Be warned, it is very dense and very rich. When I was at Lucas Carton in Paris, I was trying to make a filling for a sponge-based chocolate cake, but what came from the oven was a gloppy mess. We put the "cake" in a mold and refrigerated it to see what it might be like the next day. When my boss unmolded it and tried it, he said it was too simple to be of professional use. Meantime, I was enjoying a second helping and keeping my notes on the experiment. The cake was so rich it was like a pudding, and I knew that one day I might have use for something so simple and chocolaty.

For a dinner party, you could serve it with raspberries and perhaps some Vanilla Ice Cream (page 177). But portions should be small (even for kids).

MAKES 6 TO 8 SERVINGS

Special Equipment:
Instant-Read Thermometer; 6-Inch Round Cake Pan (See Sources, Page 225)

7 ounces (200 grams) semisweet chocolate, finely chopped

⅔ cup (162 grams) whole milk

⅓ cup (67 grams) sugar

1 large egg yolk

½ pound (2 sticks) (227 grams) unsalted butter, softened (see Note)

1 teaspoon (4 grams) pure vanilla extract

Garnish

Cocoa powder for sprinkling

1. Place the chocolate in a medium bowl and set aside.

2. Combine the milk and all but 1 tablespoon of the sugar in a small saucepan. Heat over medium heat, stirring constantly until the sugar is completely dissolved. Stop stirring and cook until the milk begins to bubble around the edge of the pan. Remove the pan from the heat.

3. Whisk together the egg yolk and the remaining 1 tablespoon sugar in a small bowl. Pour half of the hot milk over the yolk mixture, whisking to combine. Return the mixture to the saucepan and cook, whisking constantly, until the mixture thickens slightly and reaches 183°F on an instant-read thermometer.

4. Immediately pour the mixture over the chocolate. Whisk until the chocolate is melted. Add the butter ½ tablespoon at a time, whisking until the butter is melted and the mixture is smooth. Whisk in the vanilla.

5. Scrape the batter into a 6-inch round cake pan and smooth the top with a rubber spatula. Cover the pan with plastic wrap and place it in the freezer for at least 6 hours, or overnight.

6. To unmold the cake, carefully immerse the pan in hot water for a few seconds. Wipe the bottom and side of the pan dry and invert the cake onto a serving platter. Decorate the top of the cake by running a hot dull knife across its surface in a wave pattern (dip the knife in hot water and wipe completely dry before using it). Lightly dust the top of the cake with sifted cocoa powder. Allow the cake to stand at room temperature for 45 minutes before serving. Store leftovers in the refrigerator.

NOTE: It is important that the butter be at room temperature, or it will not blend completely into the chocolate mixture and there will be small lumps of butter in the cake.

You can make this two or even three days in advance and freeze it. When you need it, unmold it and let it stand at room temperature for forty-five minutes so it's not freezer cold. Or unmold it and then store in the freezer, whole or cut into portions, for up to two months.

Chocolate Pudding Cake

91

Chocolate-Pear Cake

Chocolate-Pear Cake

Chocolate Génoise

¾ cup (97 grams) cake flour, sifted

1 cup plus 1 tablespoon (100 grams) unsweetened alkalized cocoa powder, sifted

6 large eggs

1 cup (200 grams) sugar

2 tablespoons (28 grams) unsalted butter, melted

6 canned pear halves, drained and diced

Garnish

2 poached pear halves (see page 34), cut into ½-inch dice

Chocolate Sauce (page 32)

*T*he diced canned pears in this cake give it a texture similar to a moist brownie. It may surprise some people who are not expecting it. For me, the texture is sensuous, and the combination of chocolate and pear is heaven sent. Serve with chocolate sauce and, perhaps, Vanilla Ice Cream (page 177).

MAKES 6 SERVINGS

1. *Make the chocolate génoise:* Preheat the oven to 375°F. Butter an 8-inch round cake pan with a flat or decorated bottom. Dust the pan with flour and tap out the excess.

2. Whisk together the flour and cocoa powder in a medium bowl. Set aside.

3. Fill a large saucepan one-third full with water and bring to a simmer. Whisk together the eggs and sugar in the bowl of an electric mixer. Place the bowl over the simmering water, and whisk constantly until the eggs are warm to the touch. Transfer the bowl to the mixer stand and, using the whisk attachment, beat on medium speed until the mixture triples in volume, forms thick ribbons when you lift the whisk, and is cool to the touch.

4. Remove the bowl from the mixer stand and, using a large rubber spatula, gently fold in the flour mixture. Place the melted butter in a small bowl and mix in about ½ cup of the batter. Gently fold this mixture into the remaining batter. Scrape half of the batter into the prepared pan. Sprinkle the diced pears over it. Cover with the remaining batter.

5. Place the cake in the oven, lower the temperature to 350°F, and bake for 30 to 40 minutes, or until the cake begins to pull away from the side of the pan and the top springs back when lightly touched. Cool the cake in the pan for 10 minutes. Unmold the cake and cool completely.

6. *Serve the cake:* Arrange the diced poached pears in the center of the cake. Rewarm the chocolate sauce if necessary. Serve the cake with the chocolate sauce. Store, well wrapped, in the refrigerator for up to 3 days.

Chocolate Cakes

Pecan Reine de Saba

The name of this cake translates as "Queen of Sheba." Reine de Saba is exotic, but it delivers chocolate in a form that Americans love: It is really like a brownie. Although not quite as rich, it is just as chewy. My grandfather used to make this and cut it into squares like a brownie for sale in his shop. The classic recipe calls for walnuts, but I thought pecans might be an intriguing variation. It is a good recipe to play with that way. Serve it with Caramel Ice Cream (page 179).

MAKES 6 TO 8 SERVINGS

Generous 1 cup (100 grams) pecan halves

¼ cup plus 2 tablespoons (28 grams) sifted unsweetened alkalized cocoa powder

1 teaspoon (2 grams) ground cinnamon

7 tablespoons (100 grams) unsalted butter, melted and cooled

5 large eggs, separated

1¼ cups (250 grams) sugar

Pinch of salt

3 tablespoons (25 grams) cake flour, sifted

1. Preheat the oven to 350°F. Butter an 8-inch square baking pan. Dust the pan with flour and tap out the excess.

2. Place half the pecans on a baking sheet and toast in the oven for 5 to 10 minutes, shaking the pan once or twice, until the nuts are fragrant. Let the nuts cool slightly. (Leave the oven on.)

3. Place the toasted nuts in the bowl of a food processor and process until finely ground, about 45 seconds. Set aside.

4. Whisk the cocoa powder and cinnamon into the melted butter. Set aside.

5. In the bowl of an electric mixer, fitted with the whisk attachment, beat the egg yolks with ½ cup (100 grams) of the sugar at medium-high speed until thickened and pale, about 3 minutes. At low speed, mix in the cocoa mixture and ground pecans.

6. In a clean bowl of the electric mixer, using a clean whisk attachment, beat the egg whites with the salt until foamy. Gradually add the remaining ¾ cup (150 grams) sugar and beat until stiff but not dry. Gently fold the whites into the egg yolk mixture in three additions, alternating them with the cake flour in two additions. Scrape the batter into the prepared pan and sprinkle with the remaining pecans.

7. Bake for 45 to 50 minutes, until the cake springs back when lightly touched and a toothpick inserted in the center comes out with a few moist crumbs clinging to it. Cool the cake in the pan on a wire rack for 15 minutes. Unmold the cake and cool completely on the rack.

8. Cut the cake into squares to serve. Store, well wrapped, in the refrigerator for up to a week.

Pecan Reine de Saba

Chocolate-Raspberry Cake

Chocolate-Raspberry Cake

Chocolate Génoise

Scant 1 cup (120 grams) cake flour, sifted

¾ cup (56 grams) sifted unsweetened alkalized cocoa powder

6 large eggs

1 cup (200 grams) sugar

2 tablespoons (28 grams) unsalted butter, melted and cooled

Raspberry Syrup

2 tablespoons (30 grams) eau-de-framboise or other raspberry liqueur

½ cup (120 grams) Simple Syrup (page 38)

Whipped Chocolate Ganache

3½ ounces (100 grams) bittersweet chocolate, finely chopped

½ cup (116 grams) heavy cream

2 tablespoons (30 grams) eau-de-framboise or other raspberry liqueur

11 tablespoons (156 grams) unsalted butter, softened

Assembly

½ cup (150 grams) raspberry jam

*H*ere is a very simple, very basic way to enjoy the classic combination of raspberry and chocolate—chocolate génoise with a whipped chocolate ganache and raspberry jam inside. It is very rich and dense, and should be kept at room temperature so the flavors aren't muted. It doesn't need any accompaniment, though Vanilla Ice Cream (page 177) would complement the raspberry and chocolate.

MAKES 8 SERVINGS

1. *Make the chocolate génoise:* Preheat the oven to 350°F. Butter an 8½ × 4½ × 2½-inch loaf pan. Dust the pan with flour and tap out the excess.

2. Whisk together the flour and cocoa powder in a medium bowl. Set aside.

3. Fill a large saucepan one-third full with water and bring to a simmer. Whisk together the eggs and sugar in the bowl of an electric mixer. Place the bowl over the simmering water and whisk constantly until the eggs are warm to the touch. Transfer the bowl to the mixer stand and, using the whisk attachment, beat on medium speed until the mixture triples in volume, forms a thick ribbon when you lift the whisk, and is cool to the touch, about 8 minutes.

4. Remove the bowl from the mixer stand and, using a large rubber spatula, gently fold in the flour mixture. Place the melted butter in a small bowl and stir in a large spoonful of the batter until well blended. Gently fold this mixture into the remaining batter. Scrape the batter into the prepared pan and smooth the top with a spatula.

5. Bake for 30 to 35 minutes, until the cake has pulled away from the sides of the pan and the top springs back when lightly touched. Cool the

continued

*Chocolate
Cakes*

cake in the pan on a wire rack for 10 minutes. Unmold the cake and cool completely, right side up.

6. *Make the raspberry syrup:* Stir the eau-de-framboise into the simple syrup; set aside.

7. *Make the whipped chocolate ganache:* Place the chocolate in a medium bowl. Bring the cream to a boil in a small saucepan over medium-high heat. Immediately pour the hot cream over the chocolate. Gently whisk until the chocolate is completely melted and smooth. Cool to room temperature.

8. In the bowl of an electric mixer, using the whisk attachment, beat the butter at high speed until fluffy, about 3 minutes. Beat in the chocolate mixture and eau-de-framboise and beat until combined, scraping down the side of the bowl as necessary.

9. *Assemble the cake:* With a long serrated knife, carefully slice off the domed top of the cake so that it is level. Slice the cake horizontally into three equal layers. Place the bottom layer back in the clean loaf pan. Brush the cake generously with the raspberry syrup. Spread half of the raspberry jam over the cake. Scrape one third of the whipped ganache onto the jam layer and spread it into an even layer. Top with the second cake layer and press it down gently. Brush with raspberry syrup. Spread the remaining raspberry jam and then another third of the whipped ganache over the layer. Top with the remaining cake layer, pressing it down gently. Brush with the remaining raspberry syrup. Chill the cake for 20 minutes.

10. Invert the cake onto a serving platter and remove the pan. Spread the remaining ganache over the top and sides of the cake. The cake can be made up to a day ahead and refrigerated. Bring the cake to room temperature before serving.

Milk-and-Dark-Chocolate Mousse Cake

Chocolate Génoise

¾ cup plus 1 tablespoon (118 grams) all-purpose flour, sifted

¾ cup (70 grams) unsweetened alkalized cocoa powder, sifted

6 large eggs

1 cup (200 grams) sugar

2 tablespoons (28 grams) unsalted butter, melted

Milk and Dark Chocolate Mousses

3½ cups (812 grams) heavy cream

5 ounces (142 grams) milk chocolate, finely chopped

5 ounces (142 grams) bittersweet chocolate, finely chopped

Sugar Syrup

¼ cup (50 grams) sugar

Garnish

White chocolate curls (see page 21)

In my New York shop, this recipe calls for a trio of chocolate mousses, white, milk, and dark. But in order to simplify—and to give milk chocolate a chance to shine—I have eliminated the white chocolate mousse. It is a simple layer cake consisting of chocolate génoise and the mousses, with an elegant garnish of white chocolate curls.

MAKES 8 SERVINGS

Special Equipment:
9-Inch Cardboard Cake Round;
9 × 4-Inch-High Cake Ring

1. *Make the chocolate génoise:* Preheat the oven to 350°F. Butter a 9-inch round cake pan. Dust the pan with flour and tap out the excess.

2. Whisk together the flour and cocoa powder in a medium bowl; set aside.

3. Fill a pot one-third full with water and bring to a simmer. Combine the eggs and sugar in the bowl of an electric mixer. Place the bowl over the simmering water and whisk until the mixture is warm to the touch. Transfer the bowl to the mixer stand and, using the whisk attachment, beat on medium speed until the mixture triples in volume and forms a thick ribbon when the whisk is lifted, about 8 minutes. Using a large rubber spatula, gently fold in the flour mixture. Fold in the melted butter. Scrape the batter into the pan and smooth the top.

4. Bake the cake for 20 to 25 minutes, until it has pulled away from the side of the pan and the top springs back when lightly touched. Cool the cake in the pan for 10 minutes. Unmold the cake on a rack and cool completely, right side up.

5. *Make the milk and dark chocolate mousses:* In the bowl of an electric mixer, using the whisk attachment, beat 2½ cups (580 grams) of the heavy cream to soft peaks. Scrape half of the whipped cream into a medium bowl. Cover both bowls and refrigerate.

6. Put the milk and dark chocolate in two separate medium bowls. Bring the remaining 1 cup (232 grams) cream to a boil in a small sauce-

continued

*Chocolate
Cakes*

pan. Pour ½ cup (116 grams) of the hot cream over the milk chocolate and the remaining ½ cup (116 grams) over the bittersweet chocolate. Gently whisk the milk chocolate until it is completely melted and the mixture is smooth. Whisk the dark chocolate until smooth.

7. Let the chocolate mixtures cool for 10 minutes. Fold the milk chocolate mixture into one bowl of whipped cream. Fold the dark chocolate into the remaining whipped cream.

8. *Make the sugar syrup:* Combine ¼ cup (59 grams) water and the sugar in a small saucepan. Bring to a boil over medium-high heat, stirring to dissolve the sugar. Let the syrup cool to room temperature.

9. *Assemble the cake:* Using a serrated knife, slice the cake horizontally in half. Cut a strip of parchment paper to line the inside of a 9 × 4-inch cake ring. Line the mold with the strip and place it on a serving plate. Place a 9-inch cardboard cake round in the bottom of the cake ring. Place the bottom cake round, cut side up, in the ring. Brush the cake generously with the sugar syrup. Scrape the dark chocolate mousse onto the cake and smooth it into an even layer. Top with the second cake round, cut side down. Brush the cake generously with syrup. Scrape the milk chocolate mousse onto it, smoothing it into an even layer. Chill the cake for at least 2 hours and up to 24 hours.

10. To unmold the cake, lift it off the plate, holding it with your palm against the cardboard round. Using a hair dryer or warm damp towel, briefly warm the cake ring mold. Lift off the ring mold and peel off the parchment strip. Garnish the top of the cake with white chocolate curls and allow the cake to stand at room temperature for 30 minutes before serving.

Milk-and-Dark-Chocolate Mousse Cake

Chocolate-Coconut Cake

A chef visiting my kitchen happened to see our recipe for this cake, and his immediate response was, "There is something missing here!" But there is not. I had been experimenting with variations of sponge cake and devised this one, which is like a macaroon layer. A serving of this cake is like popping a coconut macaroon filled with chocolate ganache into your mouth. It is so simple that you may not believe how delicious it is until you actually try it. Serve with Vanilla Ice Cream (page 177) or Chocolate Sorbet (page 185).

MAKES 6 TO 8 SERVINGS

Coconut Sponge

4 large eggs

1½ cups (300 grams) sugar

3⅔ cups (244 grams) unsweetened dried shredded coconut

Ganache

10½ ounces (300 grams) bittersweet chocolate, finely chopped

3½ ounces (100 grams) milk chocolate, finely chopped

1⅔ cups (385 grams) heavy cream

Garnish

1 cup (80 grams) unsweetened dried shredded coconut, toasted (see page 16)

1. *Make the coconut sponge:* Preheat the oven to 350°F. Spray the bottom and sides of a 17½ × 12½-inch baking sheet with nonstick cooking spray. Line the bottom of the pan with parchment paper.

2. Fill a medium saucepan one-third full with water and bring to a simmer. Whisk together the eggs and sugar in the bowl of an electric mixer. Place the bowl over the pan of simmering water and whisk constantly until the egg mixture is warm to the touch. Transfer the bowl to the mixer stand and beat on high speed until it has tripled in volume, about 5 minutes. Using a rubber spatula, fold in the coconut just until blended. Pour the batter onto the prepared baking sheet and spread it evenly in the pan with a rubber spatula.

3. Bake for 20 to 25 minutes, until the top of the cake is light golden brown and a toothpick inserted in the center comes out clean. Cool the cake in the pan on a wire rack for 15 minutes.

4. Run a small sharp knife around the sides of the pan to loosen the cake. Place a wire rack over the cake and invert. Carefully peel off the parchment paper (the cake is extremely delicate). Cool the cake completely.

5. *Make the ganache:* Put the bittersweet and milk chocolates in a large bowl and set aside. Bring the cream to a boil in a medium saucepan. Immediately pour the hot cream over the chocolate. Whisk until the chocolate is completely melted and smooth. Cover the the ganache with plastic wrap, pressing it directly against the surface, and refrigerate until it is firm enough to pipe, about 4 hours.

Chocolate
Cakes

continued

Chocolate-Coconut Cake

6. *Assemble the cake:* Trim off any uneven edges and cut the cake crosswise into three equal rectangles, each measuring about 5 × 10 inches. Place one of the rectangles on a serving platter. Using a small metal offset spatula, spread a generous layer of ganache over the top of the cake layer. Cover with another cake layer and spread a layer of ganache over it. Top with the third cake layer and spread the remaining ganache over the top and sides of the cake. Sprinkle the toasted coconut over the top and sides of the cake. If not serving immediately, refrigerate the cake. The cake can be made up to 1 day ahead. Bring to room temperature before serving.

The staff enjoys breakfast during a break.

Chocolate Cakes

Chocolate Mikado Cake

Succès (meringue layers)

2 large eggs

1 cup (105 grams) finely ground blanched hazelnuts

1½ tablespoons (15 grams) all-purpose flour

5 large egg whites

Pinch of salt

1 cup (200 grams) sugar

Chocolate Mousse

11 ounces (312 grams) bittersweet chocolate, chopped

2 cups (464 grams) heavy cream

5 large egg yolks

½ cup (100 grams) sugar

1 tablespoon (20 grams) light corn syrup

Assembly

1⅓ cups (340 grams) Praline Paste (page 36, or see Sources, page 225)

Glaze and Garnish

1 recipe Chocolate Glaze (page 32)

2 cups (170 grams) sliced almonds, toasted (see page 16)

Chocolate cigarettes (see page 19)

1. *Make the succès layers:* Preheat the oven to 250°F. Line the bottoms of two 8-inch cake pans with rounds of parchment paper.

2. Whisk together the eggs, hazelnuts, and flour in a medium bowl; set aside.

3. In the bowl of an electric mixer, using the whisk attachment, beat the egg whites and salt at low speed until foamy. Gradually add the sugar, then beat at high speed until soft peaks form. Remove the bowl from the mixer stand and gently fold in the flour mixture. Scrape the batter into a pastry bag fitted with a ½-inch plain tip. Pipe the batter into the cake pans, starting from the outer edge and spiraling into the center of the pan; the rounds should be about ¼ inch thick.

4. Bake the rounds for 1½ to 2 hours, until they are completely dry. Set the pans on a wire rack to cool completely, then remove from the pans.

continued

M
ikado is a popular kids' game in France. It is like pick-up sticks in America. Wood sticks with numbers are tossed into a pile, and players have to pick them up one at a time without disturbing the others. We named the cake after the game because of the dense cluster of chocolate cigarettes that decorates the top, but the recipe is really an excuse to present chocolate and hazelnut, which is such an irresistible combination. Smooth mousse and crunchy cake make this cake well balanced: not too light, not too dense. Prepared in a shallow mold, with the dramatic chocolate decoration and the slivered almonds on the side, this is a delight for all the senses. Serve with Vanilla Ice Cream (page 177).

MAKES 10 SERVINGS

Special Equipment:
Pastry Bag Fitted with a ½-Inch Plain Tip (Such as Ateco #6); Candy Thermometer; 8 × 4-Inch-High Metal Cake Ring

Chocolate
Cakes

5. *Make the chocolate mousse:* Fill a large saucepan one-third full with water and bring just to a simmer. Place the chocolate in a bowl, set over the simmering water, and heat, stirring frequently, until completely melted. Set the chocolate aside to cool.

6. In the bowl of an electric mixer, using the whisk attachment, beat the heavy cream to soft peaks. Transfer to a large bowl. Cover and refrigerate.

7. In a clean mixer bowl, using the whisk attachment, begin beating the egg yolks on medium speed. Meanwhile, combine the sugar, corn syrup, and ¼ cup (59 grams) water in a medium saucepan and bring to a boil over medium-high heat, stirring to dissolve the sugar. Attach a candy thermometer to the pan and cook until the syrup reaches 243°F. Immediately, with the mixer running, pour the hot syrup down the side of the bowl into the yolks (avoid pouring the syrup onto the whisk, as it would splatter). Increase the speed to medium-high and continue beating until the eggs are doubled in volume and cool, about 7 minutes.

8. Using a rubber spatula, gently fold the melted chocolate into the whipped yolks, then fold in the whipped cream.

9. *Assemble the cake:* Line a baking sheet with parchment paper. Place an 8 × 4-inch-high ring mold on the baking sheet. Place one of the meringue layers right side up in the bottom of the mold. Using a small offset spatula, spread ⅔ cup (170 grams) of the praline paste over the layer. Scrape half of the mousse into the pan, smoothing the top with a spatula. Place the other meringue layer on top of the mousse. Spread the remaining ⅔ cup (170 grams) praline paste over the layer. Scrape the remaining chocolate mousse over the praline layer and spread it into an even layer. Place the cake in the freezer for 2 to 3 hours, until hard.

10. Remove the baking sheet from the freezer. Using a portable hair dryer or a hot damp towel, gently warm the outside of the mold. Lift up and remove the ring mold and return the cake to the freezer until ready to glaze it.

11. *Glaze and garnish the cake:* Place the cake on a cooling rack set over a baking sheet. Pour the glaze onto the center of the cake, letting it drip down the sides. Use a small offset spatula to cover the sides of the cake completely in glaze.

12. Sprinkle the top of the cake with the toasted almonds and pile the chocolate cigarettes in the center of the cake. The cake can be made up to a day in advance. Allow to stand at room temperature for 30 minutes before serving.

Chocolate Mikado Cake

Muscadine My Way

uscadine is a traditional French chocolate candy that resembles a Tootsie Roll in size and shape. It is so delicious I decided to create a version of it in cake, and I love its whimsical, rustic appearance. Chocolate and orange are the dominant flavors here—the cake is soaked in Grand Marnier syrup, and the chocolate ganache is delicately flavored with orange by incorporating candied orange peel. It is filled and formed into a tight roll, then brushed with a thin coating of melted chocolate. This surface is deliberately rough, and once the cake is rolled in confectioners' sugar, it will resemble a snow-dusted tree branch. You can make it a bit more elegant if you like, with the caramel spikes, but they are entirely optional. Serve with Vanilla Ice Cream (page 177).

MAKES 8 SERVINGS

Ganache Filling

6 ounces (170 grams) bittersweet chocolate, finely chopped

1 cup (232 grams) heavy cream

2 tablespoons (14 grams) finely chopped candied orange peel

Grand Marnier Syrup

¼ cup plus 1 tablespoon (62 grams) sugar

3 tablespoons (46 grams) Grand Marnier

Cake

4 large eggs, separated

1 cup (115 grams) confectioners' sugar

1 teaspoon (4 grams) pure vanilla extract

¼ cup plus 3 tablespoons (57 grams) cake flour

Caramel Spikes (Optional)

1 cup (200 grams) sugar

2 tablespoons (41 grams) light corn syrup

Coating

4 ounces (113 grams) bittersweet chocolate, finely chopped

½ cup (58 grams) confectioners' sugar

1. *Make the ganache filling:* Place the chocolate in a medium bowl. Bring the cream to a boil in a small saucepan. Whisk the hot cream into the chocolate until smooth and completely melted. Whisk in the orange peel. Refrigerate the ganache, stirring occasionally, for 40 minutes or until it is spreadable.

2. *Meanwhile, make the Grand Marnier syrup:* Combine the sugar and ¼ cup (59 grams) water in a small saucepan and bring to a boil, stirring to dissolve the sugar. Remove the pan from the heat and stir in the Grand Marnier. Set the syrup aside to cool to room temperature.

3. *Make the cake:* Preheat the oven to 350°F. Line a 15 × 10-inch jelly-roll pan with parchment paper, allowing the paper to extend slightly beyond the short ends of the pan.

Chocolate Cakes

continued

108

4. In the bowl of an electric mixer, using the whisk attachment, beat the egg whites at medium-low speed until foamy. Gradually add ½ cup (58 grams) of the confectioners' sugar. Increase the speed to medium-high and beat until the whites form firm, glossy peaks.

5. In a medium bowl, whisk the egg yolks by hand with ¼ cup (29 grams) of the remaining confectioners' sugar to blend. Whisk in the vanilla extract. With the mixer on low speed, add the yolk mixture to the whites and mix just until combined; do not overmix. Sift the flour over the mixture and, using a large rubber spatula, gently fold it in. Scrape the batter into the prepared pan and smooth the top. Sprinkle the cake with 2 tablespoons (14 grams) of the remaining confectioners' sugar. Let it stand for 5 minutes.

6. Sprinkle the cake with the remaining 2 tablespoons (14 grams) confectioners' sugar. Bake the cake for 10 to 12 minutes, until the top is light golden and springs back when lightly touched. Slide the cake, on the parchment paper, onto a rack, and cool to room temperature.

7. Place a sheet of parchment paper on a work surface and invert the cake onto the paper. Peel off the top sheet of parchment paper. Brush the Grand Marnier syrup over the cake. Using an offset metal spatula, spread the ganache filling evenly over the cake. Starting from one of the short ends of the cake, using the paper for assistance, roll up the cake into a log. Place the log on a platter or baking sheet; cover with plastic wrap and refrigerate for 1 hour.

8. *Meanwhile, make the optional caramel spikes:* Combine the sugar, corn syrup, and ¼ cup (59 grams) water in a small saucepan. Bring to a boil over medium heat, stirring to dissolve the sugar. Boil until the syrup is a light caramel color, about 5 minutes. (To avoid burns, be very cautious when handling hot caramel.) Remove the pan from the heat and let cool for 5 minutes.

9. Line a baking sheet with parchment paper. Drop a small spoonful of the syrup onto the paper, making a pool ½ inch in diameter. Using a small offset metal spatula or a knife, starting at the center of the dot, draw the caramel out to shape a spike or plume. Continue to shape about 7 spikes. Refrigerate until firm, about 15 minutes.

10. *Just before serving, coat the cake:* Fill a medium saucepan one-third full with water and bring to a simmer. Place the chocolate in a medium bowl, set it over the water, and heat until melted, stirring occasionally. Remove from the heat.

11. Spread the confectioners' sugar on a baking sheet. Brush the cold cake with the melted chocolate, then roll it in the confectioners' sugar to coat completely. Return the cake to the refrigerator for 5 minutes to set the chocolate, then transfer it to a serving platter. If desired, stand a few caramel spikes up on the cake. The cake can be made up to a day ahead and refrigerated. Bring the cake to room temperature before serving.

My parents steal a kiss from me in front of their pâtisserie.

JEAN MARIE DEL MORAL

Chocolate Cakes

Chocolate Charlotte

Chocolate Charlotte

Ladyfingers

5 large eggs, separated, at room temperature

¼ cup (50 grams) granulated sugar

1 teaspoon (4 grams) pure vanilla extract

1 cup (115 grams) confectioners' sugar, plus more for dusting the ladyfingers

Scant 1 cup (120 grams) cake flour

Cocoa Syrup

¼ cup (50 grams) sugar

1 tablespoon (6 grams) unsweetened alkalized cocoa powder, sifted

Chocolate Mousse

2 cups (464 grams) heavy cream

12 ounces (340 grams) extra-bittersweet chocolate, chopped

3 large eggs

3 large egg yolks

⅔ cup (134 grams) sugar

I grew up with this, my father's variation of a classic charlotte. Most charlotte recipes involve lining the mold with ladyfingers or sponge cake, then filling it with layers of custard, fruit, and/or whipped cream. My father preferred chocolate mousse, which is denser than the familiar custard, and he reinforced the flavor by soaking the ladyfingers in cocoa syrup. He used the traditional charlotte mold for this, but if you don't have one, a soufflé mold is fine. When the charlotte is finished, the final touch is to pipe floral ovals of mousse along its edge—a real crowd pleaser.

MAKES 10 SERVINGS

Special Equipment:
Pastry Bag Fitted with a ½-Inch Plain Tip (Such as Ateco #6); Candy Thermometer; 4-Inch-High Charlotte Mold (or Soufflé Mold); Pastry Bag Fitted with a ½-Inch St.-Honoré Tip

1. *Make the ladyfingers:* Preheat the oven to 375°F. Cut two pieces of parchment paper to line two baking sheets. Draw two 6-inch circles on one of the sheets. Draw two 4-inch-wide (or the height of your mold) × 12-inch-long rectangles next to each other on the other piece. Turn each piece of paper over and place one on each baking sheet.

2. In the bowl of an electric mixer, using the whisk attachment, beat the egg yolks and granulated sugar at high speed until the mixture is pale and forms a thick ribbon when the whisk is lifted. Blend in the vanilla extract.

3. In a clean dry mixer bowl, using the cleaned whisk attachment, begin beating the egg whites on low speed until foamy. Increase the speed to medium and gradually add the confectioners' sugar. Increase the speed to high and beat just until stiff peaks form. Sift half of the cake flour over the yolk mixture, then gently fold in the meringue until just combined. Repeat with the remaining cake flour.

4. Fill a pastry bag fitted with a ½-inch plain tip with the batter. Pipe 4-inch-long (or whatever the height of your mold is) ladyfingers side by side in the rectangles you traced onto the sheet of parchment; pipe them very close to each other so that they will bake together and form a band. Pipe two 6-inch rounds onto the other baking sheet, starting from the outside edge of each traced circle and spiraling toward the center.

5. Sift confectioners' sugar over the ladyfingers and bake until golden

continued

brown, 7 to 10 minutes. Slide the parchment paper onto wire racks and cool the ladyfinger bands and rounds, then sprinkle them again with sifted confectioners' sugar.

6. *Make the cocoa syrup:* Whisk together the ½ cup (118 grams) water, sugar, and cocoa powder in a small saucepan. Bring to a boil over medium-high heat, whisking until the sugar is dissolved. Let the syrup cool to room temperature.

7. *Make the chocolate mousse:* In the bowl of an electric mixer, using the whisk attachment, beat the heavy cream to soft peaks. Transfer to a large bowl and refrigerate until ready to use.

8. Fill a large saucepan one-third full with water and bring to a simmer. Place the chocolate in a bowl set over the simmering water and heat, stirring frequently until the chocolate is melted. Cool until tepid.

9. Meanwhile, in a clean mixer bowl, using the whisk attachment, begin beating the eggs and egg yolks at medium speed. As the eggs are beating, combine the sugar and 2 tablespoons (30 grams) water in a medium heavy saucepan and bring to a boil over medium-high heat, stirring to dissolve the sugar. Boil the syrup, without stirring, until it registers 243°F on a candy thermometer. Turn the mixer to low speed and pour the hot syrup over the yolks. Increase the speed to medium-high and beat the eggs until they have doubled in volume and are cool, about 8 minutes.

10. Fold the warm melted chocolate into the whipped cream. Gently fold in the beaten yolk mixture.

11. *Assemble the charlotte:* Line a 6 × 4-inch-high charlotte or soufflé mold with plastic wrap. Line the bottom of the mold with ladyfingers by separating some from one of the bands and arranging them in a flower-petal pattern. Cover the bottom of the mold completely, trimming the ladyfingers as necessary to fit snugly in the mold. Line the side of the mold with the remaining ladyfinger bands, sugared side out, cutting the bands as necessary to fit the mold. Fill the mold half-full with chocolate mousse. Place one of the ladyfinger rounds on top of the mousse. Fill the mold to within ¼ inch of the top with more mousse and place the other ladyfinger round on top, sugared side up. Refrigerate the charlotte and the remaining chocolate mousse for at least 2 hours and up to 24 hours.

12. To unmold the charlotte, dip the bottom of the mold in hot water for a few seconds, dry it, and invert the charlotte onto a serving plate. Remove the plastic wrap. Remove the remaining mousse from the refrigerator and stir it. Scrape the mousse into a pastry bag fitted with a ½-inch St.-Honoré tip. Pipe quenelles of the mousse around the top of the charlotte in a flower pattern. The charlotte can be made up to a day ahead and refrigerated. Let stand at room temperature for 30 minutes before serving.

Ladyfingers

Gâteau Alexandra

I created this for my wife because she loves a cake with a crunchy interior. Since it was to be named for her, I wanted to be sure that it was elegant and memorable as well. It is oval in shape, and consists of three layers of baked chocolate Swiss meringue, filled with chocolate mousse and decorated with "fingers" of meringue. You can add a layer of raspberry jam for a bit of acidity and color, if you care to. Serve with Vanilla Ice Cream (page 177).

MAKES 6 TO 8 SERVINGS

Special Equipment:
Pastry Bag Fitted with a ½-Inch Plain Tip (Such as Ateco #6); Candy Thermometer

Chocolate Cakes

Chocolate Swiss Meringue

8 large egg whites

1¼ cups (250 grams) sugar

¾ cup plus 1 tablespoon (77 grams) unsweetened alkalized cocoa powder, sifted

Chocolate Mousse

2 large eggs

1 large egg yolk

⅓ cup (66 grams) sugar

6 ounces (170 grams) bittersweet chocolate, chopped

1 cup (232 grams) heavy cream

Garnish

Confectioners' sugar for sprinkling

1. *Make the chocolate Swiss meringue:* Arrange two racks near the center of the oven and preheat the oven to 250°F. Line two 17½ × 12½-inch baking sheets with parchment paper. Draw three 8½ × 5-inch ovals on one of the sheets of paper and turn the paper over.

2. Fill a large pot one-third full with water and bring to a simmer. Whisk together the egg whites and sugar in the bowl of an electric mixer. Place the bowl over the simmering water and whisk constantly until the whites are warm to the touch. Transfer the bowl to the mixer stand and, using the whisk attachment, beat the whites on high speed until they form stiff peaks. Remove the bowl from the stand and, using a large rubber spatula, gently fold in the cocoa powder.

3. Fill a pastry bag fitted with a ½-inch plain tip with the chocolate meringue. Using the traced outlines as a guide, pipe three ovals onto the baking sheet, piping from the edge to the center of each oval in a spiral pattern. On the other baking sheet, pipe out as many 3 × ¾-inch-wide "fingers" of meringue as you can.

4. Bake, switching the pans halfway through the baking time, for about 2½ hours, until the meringues are crisp. Cool the meringues on the baking sheets.

5. *Make the chocolate mousse:* In the bowl of an electric mixer fitted with the whisk attachment, beat the eggs and egg yolk on medium-high speed. Meanwhile, combine the sugar and 1½ tablespoons (22 grams) water in a small saucepan and bring to a boil over high heat, stirring until

continued

Gâteau Alexandra

the sugar is dissolved. Insert a candy thermometer into the pan and cook the syrup until it registers 243°F. Immediately remove the pan from the heat, reduce the mixer speed to low, and pour the syrup onto the egg yolks (avoid pouring the syrup onto the whisk, as it would splatter). Increase the speed to medium-high and beat the yolks until they have doubled in volume and are almost cool, about 5 minutes.

6. Fill a large saucepan one-third full with water and bring to a simmer. Place the chocolate in a bowl set over the simmering water and heat, stirring frequently, until the chocolate is melted. Cool until tepid.

7. In a clean mixer bowl, with the whisk attachment, beat the heavy cream on high speed until soft peaks form. Fold the melted chocolate into the whipped yolks, then gently fold in the whipped cream. Transfer 1½ cups of the mousse to a small bowl and set it aside for frosting the cake.

8. *Assemble the cake:* If necessary, gently trim the meringue ovals with a sharp paring knife so they are uniform. Place one of the meringue ovals on a serving plate. Spread half of the mousse onto it in an even layer. Place a second oval on top and spread with another half of the mousse. Place the third oval on top. Refrigerate the cake for 20 minutes.

9. Spread the reserved 1½ cups mousse over the top and sides of the cake. Cover the sides of the cake with meringue fingers, placing them on a diagonal and pressing them lightly so that they adhere. Chop the remaining fingers into ½-inch pieces and scatter them over the top of the cake. Sprinkle the cake with sifted confectioners' sugar. The cake can be made up to 1 day in advance and refrigerated. Allow to stand at room temperature for 30 minutes before serving.

Hedgehog Cake

Chocolate Sponge

½ pound (2 sticks) (237 grams) unsalted butter, cut into tablespoons

9 ounces (255 grams) bittersweet chocolate, finely chopped

5 large eggs separated

½ cup (100 grams) sugar

1 tablespoon (9 grams) all-purpose flour

Pinch of salt

Chestnut Ganache

13 ounces (368 grams) extra-bittersweet chocolate, finely chopped

2 cups (464 grams) heavy cream

1½ cups (408 grams) sweetened chestnut purée (see Sources, page 225)

Whipped Cream Filling

⅓ cup (77 grams) heavy cream

Garnish

Cocoa powder for dusting

1. *Make the chocolate sponge:* Preheat the oven to 350°F. Spray the bottom and sides of a 17½ × 12½-inch baking sheet with nonstick cooking spray and line the bottom with parchment paper.

2. Fill a medium saucepan one-third full with water and bring to a simmer. Put the butter and chocolate in a medium bowl, place the bowl over the simmering water and heat, stirring occasionally, until the butter and chocolate are completely melted and the mixture is smooth. Remove the bowl from the pan and allow the chocolate mixture to cool.

3. Whisk together the egg yolks, ¼ cup (50 grams) of the sugar, and the flour in a medium bowl until pale. Set aside.

4. In the bowl of an electric mixer, using the whisk attachment, beat the egg whites and salt at medium speed until frothy. Gradually add the remaining ¼ cup (50 grams) sugar and beat at high speed until soft peaks form.

5. Whisk the chocolate mixture into the yolk mixture. Using a large rubber spatula, gently fold in the beaten whites. Scrape the batter into the prepared pan and smooth the top with the spatula.

6. Bake the cake for 25 to 30 minutes, until it pulls away from the sides of the pan and a toothpick inserted in the center of the cake comes out clean. Cool the cake completely in the pan.

This cake evolved from a project I assigned myself: to look for animals that I could model desserts after. It consists of layers of chocolate sponge and chocolate chestnut ganache, with a layer of whipped cream to alleviate the density and to add visual interest. The cake is assembled in a bowl to give it its round shape. Then it's unmolded and covered with more ganache. The "spikes" are created from the ganache—try to make them as high as you can. Kids will love the cake, but you will want to keep the portions small. This hedgehog is best served by itself.

MAKES 12 SERVINGS

Special Equipment:
8-Inch-Wide Stainless Steel Bowl

*Chocolate
Cakes*

continued

Hedgehog Cake

7. Using a paring knife and plates or lids as guides, cut 3 discs, one measuring 5 inches in diameter, one 6 inches, and one 7 inches, from the cake; leave the discs on the baking sheet.

8. *Make the chestnut ganache:* Put the chocolate in a medium bowl. Bring the heavy cream to a boil in a medium saucepan. Immediately pour the hot cream over the chocolate. Whisk until the chocolate is completely melted and the mixture is smooth.

9. Place the chestnut purée in a large bowl. Gradually whisk in the chocolate mixture, whisking until smooth. Transfer 1¼ cups (327 grams) of the ganache to a small bowl for garnishing the dessert. Cover both bowls with plastic wrap and refrigerate, stirring occasionally, until the ganache is firm enough to pipe, about 45 minutes.

10. *Make the whipped cream filling:* In the bowl of an electric mixer, using the whisk attachment, beat the cream to stiff peaks.

11. *Assemble the cake:* Line an 8-inch-wide bowl with plastic wrap. Scrape 1 cup of the chestnut ganache into the bowl. Using a small offset metal spatula, spread the ganache evenly over the interior of the bowl. Using a metal spatula, carefully transfer the 5-inch cake disc to the bottom of the bowl, pressing it lightly into the ganache. Spread ⅓ cup (87 grams) of the ganache over the cake disc. Carefully place the 6-inch disc over the ganache-covered disc. Spread another ⅓ cup of the ganache over the cake disc. Scrape the whipped cream filling over the ganache and spread it into an even layer. Carefully place the 7-inch disc over the cream layer and spread with the remaining ganache. Cover the bowl with plastic wrap and freeze the cake for at least 2 hours and up to 3 days.

12. To unmold the cake, carefully immerse the bowl in hot water for several seconds, then invert the cake onto a serving plate. Frost the cake with the reserved 1¼ cups ganache. Using the back of a spoon or a small spatula, pull out spikes of ganache from the cake. Sprinkle the cake with sifted cocoa powder.

Tarts and Tartlets

The recipes in this chapter are a mix of classic tarts I love and variations I've devised over the years. The variations include several individual tarts, which is the way tarts are often served in fine restaurants today and is a nice way to serve desserts at home.

Americans are more familiar with pie. One of the crucial differences between a pie and a tart is the dough. Pie dough is generally flaky, whereas French tart dough is crisp and firm. Almost all of the tarts in this chapter are made from the same sweet tart dough, *pâte sucrée*. Prepared in a food processor, this dough is very, very simple to make.

Tarts are simple, but with all the great fruit available to us, a tart should always be amazing. Apricots, peaches, apples, and berries in all their juicy, sweet-tart glory—to place such fruit as the centerpiece of a tart is to honor it. And if there is no fresh fruit at the market, there is always chocolate.

Most tarts should not be served straight out of the oven; it is best to allow them to cool to room temperature. Many of the tarts included here are fine plain, but if you want to accompany them with something, choose a complementary sauce, ice cream, or sorbet; nothing too shocking or contrasting. Crème anglaise is perfect with many of these recipes. In France, tarts in particular, and pastry in general, are so popular that you can walk into any shop and buy fresh crème anglaise or a fruit sauce to go. Too bad it is not so in America (perhaps if these tarts catch on, there will be a business opportunity for you).

Tartes Tatin

⅔ cup (134 grams) sugar

1 tablespoon (14 grams) unsalted butter

4 medium (680 grams) Granny Smith apples

1 sheet (½ of a 17¼-ounce package) frozen puff pastry, thawed

1. Preheat the oven to 350°F. Arrange four 3 × 2-inch-high aluminum foil or metal molds on a baking sheet.

2. Combine the sugar with 3 tablespoons (44 grams) water in a medium saucepan. Bring to a boil over medium-high heat, stirring until the sugar is dissolved. Wash down the sides of the pan with a wet pastry brush. Boil without stirring until the caramel reaches a golden amber color. Remove the pan from the heat and stir in the butter (stand back as the caramel will bubble up and may splatter).

3. Divide the hot caramel among the molds (there should be about ¼ inch of caramel on the bottom of each mold). Allow the caramel to cool to room temperature.

4. Peel and core the apples. Slice off the bottom of each apple so that it stands upright. Cut each apple into 10 wedges, keeping the apple slices together. "Reassemble" the slices of 1 apple in each mold, with the bottom of the apple against the caramel. Bake the apples for 55 minutes, or until they are soft but not mushy. Remove the baking sheet from the oven and set the apples aside while you bake the pastry.

5. Increase the oven temperature to 400°F. On a floured surface, roll the puff pastry sheet out to a ⅛-inch thickness. Using a biscuit cutter, cut out four 3¼-inch rounds from the puff pastry. Place the rounds on a parchment-lined baking sheet and prick them well with a fork. Bake the rounds for 12 to 15 minutes, until puffed and golden brown. Set aside in warm place. Reduce the oven temperature to 350°F.

6. Push the apples down a bit in the molds. Reheat the apples for about 8 minutes, until the caramel is liquid and bubbling. Place a baked pastry round on top of each apple. To unmold the tarts, slip a potholder under one of the molds, place an inverted dessert plate over the pastry round, and immediately invert the tart onto the dessert plate, being careful to avoid getting the hot caramel on your hands. Repeat with the remaining tarts.

*T*arte Tatin is traditionally made with caramelized apples baked under a short dough crust in a shallow baking dish; it is then turned over when served, so that the caramelized apples are on top. This individual-serving variation is a simplified version of the classic, and it is not as heavy. I like to use puff pastry rather than the rich tart dough.

This is best served right out of the oven, hot on the outside and the apples just warm on the inside. If you must make it the night before, the puff pastry will suffer. Rewarm it for six or seven minutes before serving, and some of its flakiness will be restored. Serve this with rum raisin or Vanilla Ice Cream (page 177). At Payard, we make other variations too, including apple and apricot and apple and banana.

MAKES 4 SERVINGS

Special Equipment:
Four 3 × 2-Inch-High Aluminum Foil or Metal Molds; 3¼-Inch Biscuit Cutter

*Tarts
and
Tartlets*

Lemon Tart

Pastry chefs sometimes tend to make things too complex, and this perfect, perfectly simple lemon tart proves that complexity is unnecessary. When I first started making it, both customers and staff agreed that it was better than the labor-intensive tart we were serving in the shop at the time. And some chefs are afraid of tartness. But when people want lemon, they don't want to eat a bowl of sugar. With this tart, you taste the lemon. It is perfectly balanced between the sweet and sour. You want the richness of the lemon without it being too acid, and the rich buttery crust cuts the acidity too.

Most lemon tart recipes are made with lemon curd, which involves a lot of cooking, but this is a streamlined version. The tart shell can be made the day before, and so can the filling, but they should be stored separately.

MAKES 6 TO 8 SERVINGS

Special Equipment:
Channel Knife

Grated zest and juice of 3 lemons

3 large eggs

½ cup plus 1 tablespoon (112 grams) sugar

3 tablespoons (43 grams) unsalted butter, cut into ½-inch pieces

One 9½-inch tart shell made from Sweet Tart Dough (page 26), prebaked

Garnish

1 lemon

¼ cup (60 grams) Apricot Glaze (page 33)

Mint leaves

1. Preheat the oven to 325°F.

2. Fill a medium saucepan one-third full with water and bring to a simmer. Put the zest and lemon juice in a medium bowl and whisk in the eggs. Add the sugar and butter and place the bowl over the simmering water; the water must not touch the bottom of the bowl. Cook, whisking constantly, until the butter is completely melted and the mixture is smooth. Remove the bowl from the pan of hot water and allow the mixture to cool for 15 minutes.

3. Place the prebaked tart shell on a baking sheet. Pour the filling into the shell and bake the tart for 8 to 10 minutes, or until the center is just set. Cool the tart completely on a wire rack.

4. *Make the garnish:* Using a channel knife, cut 6 lengthwise grooves in the lemon, removing 6 strips of rind. Cut a crosswise slice from the center of the lemon and place it in the center of the tart. Slice the remaining lemon halves lengthwise in half and then cut the sections into half-moons. Arrange the slices around the edge of the tart with the cut sides out.

5. If necessary, rewarm the apricot glaze over low heat or in the microwave. Using a pastry brush, lightly brush the top of the tart with the warm apricot glaze. Garnish with a few mint leaves.

*Tarts
and
Tartlets*

Lemon Tart

Coconut-Pineapple Tart

Coconut-Pineapple Tart

½ cup (85 grams) diced fresh or canned pineapple, drained

One 9½-inch tart shell made from Sweet Tart Dough (page 26), unbaked

7 tablespoons (100 grams) unsalted butter, softened

1 cup (200 grams) sugar

2½ cups (200 grams) unsweetened dried shredded coconut

2 large eggs

Confectioners' sugar

1. Preheat the oven to 350°F.

2. Scatter the pineapple pieces over the bottom of the tart shell, gently pressing them into the dough. Place the tart shell in the freezer for 5 minutes.

3. In the bowl of an electric mixer fitted with the paddle attachment, beat the butter and sugar on medium speed for 1 minute, or until well blended. Beat in the coconut and then beat in the eggs one at a time, mixing well after each addition. Spread the filling evenly in the tart shell.

4. Bake the tart 50 to 55 minutes, until the top is a deep golden brown and the center of the tart is set. Cool the tart completely on a wire rack and dust with confectioners' sugar before serving. Refrigerate the tart if not serving immediately. Bring to room temperature before serving.

This is like a piña colada in tart form. I have always loved coconut and pineapple. Though it will work with canned pineapple, the acidity of a fresh pineapple is different from that found in the canned variety. If you are using fresh pineapple, make sure you drain it; there is a great deal of water in fresh pineapple. Putting the tart shell in the freezer for five minutes or so to chill the pineapple ensures that when you spread the coconut filling, the pineapple won't slide all over the tart shell. That way, when you slice it, the layers will be beautiful and distinct.

To remove a tart ring, place the tart on a smaller surface, such as a coffee can, and gently press down on the ring until it detaches.

MAKES 6 SERVINGS

Rustic Peach Tart

A peach is such a perfect creation of nature that it demands to be treated in a simple manner. This recipe will work with any kind of peach, white or yellow, but must be made with ripe peaches. Don't expect baking to improve unripe fruit. When you bake a ripe peach, its distinct flavor becomes slightly acidic and you will see it brown, even blacken on top. That is why I call this a rustic tart. I make a point of putting this tart in the window of my New York shop because the color reflecting the sun in the window draws customers inside. It may have a similar effect at your table. Serve with Vanilla Ice Cream (page 177) or Crème Anglaise (page 31).

MAKES 6 TO 8 SERVINGS

1 cup (210 grams) Almond Cream (page 29)

One 9½-inch tart shell made from Sweet Tart Dough (page 26); prebaked

5 to 6 ripe peaches, quartered and pitted

¼ cup (60 grams) Apricot Glaze (page 33)

1. Preheat the oven to 350°F.

2. Scrape the almond cream into the tart shell and spread it into an even layer. Arrange the peaches, cut side up, in a pinwheel pattern over the filling, starting from the edge of the tart and working toward the center.

3. Bake for 35 to 40 minutes, until the filling is set. Cool the tart on a wire rack.

4. If necessary, rewarm the apricot glaze over low heat or in the microwave. Using a pastry brush, lightly brush the top of the tart with the glaze. The tart can be made up to 1 day in advance and stored in the refrigerator. Bring to room temperature before serving.

Rustic Peach Tart

Apricot-Almond-Raspberry Tart

Apricot-Almond-Raspberry Tart

9 tablespoons (128 grams) unsalted butter, melted

7 fresh or canned apricots, cut into thirds and pitted

½ cup plus 2 tablespoons (125 grams) sugar

1 cup (210 grams) Almond Cream (page 29)

One 9½-inch tart shell made from Sweet Tart Dough (page 26), prebaked

½ pint (113 grams) raspberries

2 tablespoons (15 grams) slivered almonds

2 tablespoons (19 grams) chopped pistachios

1. Preheat the oven to 350°F.

2. Brush a baking sheet with some of the melted butter. Arrange the apricots, cut side up, on the sheet and brush with the remaining melted butter. Sprinkle the apricots with the sugar. Bake for 10 to 12 minutes, until tender. Set the apricots aside to cool on the baking sheet. (Leave the oven on.)

3. Scrape half of the almond cream into the tart shell and smooth it into an even layer. Sprinkle the raspberries over the almond cream and push them lightly into the cream. Arrange the apricots, cut side up, in a pinwheel pattern over the raspberries, starting from the edge and working toward the center. Scrape the remaining almond cream over the fruit and spread it into an even layer. Sprinkle the almonds and pistachios over the top.

4. Bake the tart for 25 to 27 minutes, until the filling is golden brown. Cool the tart completely on a wire rack. The tart can be made up to 1 day in advance and refrigerated. Bring to room temperature before serving.

This is the perfect tart to take on a picnic. I make this for my wife and a friend whenever they go to Central Park for a concert or play. The almond cream keeps it very moist. It works with canned apricots but, of course, if you can get fresh apricots, do so. Apricots have a reputation of being bland, because so many people only know the canned variety. But believe me, when an apricot is baked, it is anything but bland. The blended acidity of raspberries and apricots is so vibrant you will feel palpitations from it on your tongue. This is best by itself, but if you want, you can serve it with Vanilla Ice Cream (page 177).

MAKES 6 TO 8 SERVINGS

Fig Tart

*I*f I had to pick a favorite recipe in this book, this might be it. Certainly, at least a finalist. I love figs. In our garden we had a fig tree, and I grew up playing with them like toys—smashing them up, having them with vanilla ice cream. It is too bad that they are so expensive today, because I still like to play with them: I sauté figs in butter and serve them with mascarpone ice cream, fromage blanc ice cream, even goat cheese ice cream. Figs are a great fruit to add to a cheese plate. I sometimes poach figs in wine, which is amazing, but for this tart I kept it simple. It is just figs and almond cream, so that the flavor of the figs is the star. When it cooks, a fig retains all its moisture, and a very distinct flavor emerges from the heat. In America, we are lucky to have Black Mission figs from California; they are outstanding. This tart can be served warm or cold, with Vanilla Ice Cream (page 177).

MAKES 6 TO 8 SERVINGS

21 figs, preferably Black Mission

1½ cups (315 grams) Almond Cream (page 29)

One 9½-inch tart shell made from Sweet Tart Dough (page 26), prebaked

¼ cup (60 grams) Apricot Glaze (page 33)

1. Preheat the oven to 325°F.

2. Remove the stems from the figs. Quarter 15 of the figs and set aside. Cut the remaining figs in half and place them in the bowl of a food processor and process until puréed.

3. Scrape the almond cream into the tart shell and spread into an even layer. Spread the fig purée evenly over the almond cream. Arrange the quartered figs, skin side down, in a pinwheel pattern on the purée, starting from the edge of the tart and working toward the center.

4. Bake the tart for 30 to 35 minutes, until the filling is golden brown. Cool the tart on a wire rack for 10 minutes.

5. If necessary, rewarm the glaze over low heat or in the microwave. Using a pastry brush, lightly brush the top of the tart with the glaze. Serve warm or cold. The tart can be made up to 1 day in advance and refrigerated.

Tarts
and
Tartlets

Fig Tart

Rhubarb-Streusel Tart

Rhubarb-Streusel Tart

Streusel

7 tablespoons (100 grams) unsalted butter, softened

½ cup (100 grams) sugar

1 cup (88 grams) almond flour (see Sources, page 225)

⅔ cup (97 grams) all-purpose flour

Filling

1¼ pounds (about 9 medium stalks) (570 grams) rhubarb, washed, trimmed, peeled, and cut into ¾-inch pieces

½ cup plus 1 tablespoon (112 grams) sugar

Juice of 6 oranges

2 tablespoons (28 grams) unsalted butter

2 tablespoons (18 grams) all-purpose flour

One 9½-inch tart shell made from Sweet Tart Dough (page 26), partially baked

1. *Make the streusel:* In the bowl of an electric mixer fitted with the paddle attachment, beat the butter and sugar at high speed until light and fluffy, about 1 minute. Add the almond and all-purpose flours and mix on low speed just until combined. Set aside at room temperature.

2. *Make the filling:* Combine the rhubarb, ½ cup (100 grams) of the sugar, the orange juice, and butter in a large saucepan. Bring to a boil over medium-high heat. Reduce the heat and simmer until the rhubarb is tender but still holds its shape, about 5 minutes (don't overcook the rhubarb, or it will be mushy). Transfer the filling to a medium bowl and refrigerate until cool.

3. Preheat the oven to 350°F.

4. Stir together the flour and the remaining 1 tablespoon (12 grams) sugar in a small bowl. Sprinkle over the bottom of the tart shell. Drain the rhubarb, discarding the liquid, and spoon the filling into the tart shell.

5. Bake for 30 to 35 minutes, until the pastry is golden around the edges. Place the tart on an insulated baking sheet (or two regular baking sheets stacked together), sprinkle the streusel mixture over the tart and bake for 10 to 12 minutes longer, until the topping is lightly browned. Cool the tart slightly on a wire rack and serve, or let cool completely before serving.

*R*hubarb is one of my favorite vegetables. I use it a lot—in a soup (see page 44), in a cake, and in this tart, which is a bestseller in my shop. People like the slight tartness of it. The acidity of the sweeter orange juice goes well with the acidity of the rhubarb. You boil them together, but only for five minutes—just until the rhubarb is "imprinted" with the orange flavor. If you cook it too long, you will lose the texture of the rhubarb. This tart will keep in the refrigerator for up to three days. Serve warm or at room temperature with Vanilla Ice Cream (page 177).

MAKES 6 TO 8 SERVINGS

Rum-Raisin Almond Tart

This is a very distinctive tart. Almost like a rum cake in flavor, but with a cakey-crunchy texture all its own, it creates a memorable flavor sensation in your mouth. This is due to the exceptional moistness of the almond cream in the center, the crunchiness of the dough, and the faint orange note created by the rum-soaked raisins in combination with the almond. I used to make this as a petit four, but without the top tart shell. You can also make this without the top tart shell, but it is much more enticing the way we present it here. The tart can be frozen, and it will keep in the refrigerator for a week if you wrap it well. Rewarm a slice in the microwave for a few seconds, and it will be as good as just baked.

MAKES 6 SERVINGS

Special Equipment:
9-Inch Tart Ring

Tart

½ cup (90 grams) golden raisins

¼ cup plus 2 tablespoons (82 grams) dark rum, such as Myers's

1 recipe Sweet Tart Dough (page 26)

2 cups (420 grams) Almond Cream (page 29)

¼ cup (60 grams) Apricot Glaze (page 33)

Glaze

3 tablespoons (21 grams) confectioners' sugar

1. *Make the tart:* Place the raisins and ¼ cup (55 grams) of the rum in an airtight container and let soak for at least 8 hours, or overnight.

2. Preheat the oven to 350°F. Arrange two baking racks near the center of the oven.

3. On a lightly floured surface, roll the dough into a rectangle about 10 × 20 inches, with a thickness of ⅛ inch. Using a 9-inch tart ring as a guide, cut out two 9-inch circles from the dough with a paring knife. Place one circle on a baking sheet and place the other dough circle in the tart ring on another baking sheet.

4. Drain the raisins and transfer to a medium bowl. Stir in the almond cream. Scrape the mixture onto the dough round inside the metal ring, spreading it into an even layer. Place the plain round on the higher oven rack and the filled tart round on the lower rack. Bake for 15 to 17 minutes, until the plain round is golden brown around the edge. Remove this round to a wire baking rack to cool, and continue to bake the filled tart round for 18 to 20 minutes longer, until the top is golden brown and a toothpick inserted in the center comes out clean. Place the tart on a wire rack. (Leave the oven on.)

5. With a pastry brush, brush the remaining 2 tablespoons (27 grams) rum over the top of the warm tart.

6. If necessary, rewarm the apricot glaze over low heat or in the microwave. Lightly brush the top of the tart with the glaze. Place the plain tart round on top.

7. *Glaze the tart:* Whisk the confectioners' sugar with 1 teaspoon (5 grams) water in a small bowl until smooth. Pour the glaze onto the center of the tart and spread it over the top with the back of a spoon. Place the tart in the oven for 5 minutes, or until the glaze melts and is transparent around the edges but still slightly opaque in the center. Cool the tart on a wire rack. Remove the tart ring before serving.

Rum-Raisin Almond Tart

Caramel-Walnut Tart

Caramel-Walnut Tart

⅔ cup (133 grams) sugar

1¼ cups (142 grams) chopped walnuts

½ cup (116 grams) heavy cream

One 9½-inch tart shell made from Sweet Tart Dough (page 26), unbaked

1 cup (210 grams) Almond Cream (page 29)

3 tablespoons (45 grams) Apricot Glaze (page 33)

Confectioners' sugar for sprinkling

*T*arts with nuts and caramel are so popular in my shop, it seems that there can never be enough variations to satisfy all my customers. This straightforward pairing is just chewy enough to allow you to savor the harmony of caramel and walnut, with almond cream providing moisture and an echo of the featured flavors. The tart can be made up to 3 days in advance and refrigerated. Bring to room temperature before serving. Serve with Vanilla Ice Cream (page 177).

MAKES 6 SERVINGS

1. Have ready a large baking pan, such as a 9 × 13-inch pan. Combine the sugar and 2 tablespoons (30 grams) water in a medium saucepan. Bring to a boil over medium-high heat, stirring until the sugar is dissolved. Wash down the sides of the pan with a wet pastry brush. Boil without stirring until the syrup turns a golden amber color. Remove the pan from the heat and add the chopped walnuts. Stir for 20 seconds, or until the walnuts are slightly toasted and completely coated. Stir in the heavy cream (stand back—the caramel will bubble up and may splatter). Return the pan to the heat and cook, stirring constantly, until any lumps have disappeared and the mixture is smooth. Pour into the baking pan. Put the baking pan in the refrigerator until cool, about 20 minutes.

2. Preheat the oven to 350°F.

3. Scrape the cooled caramel mixture into the tart shell and spread into an even layer. Spread the almond cream over the caramel layer, smoothing it with a spatula.

4. Bake the tart for 35 to 40 minutes, until the top is golden brown. Cool the tart in the pan on a wire rack.

5. If necessary, rewarm the apricot glaze. Brush the warm glaze over the top of the tart. Allow the glaze to cool for 20 minutes. Immediately before serving, place a doily or cake decorating stencil (see page 225 for mail order sources) on top of the tart and sprinkle generously with confectioners' sugar. Carefully remove the stencil.

Tarts
and
Tartlets

Hazelnut Tart with Chocolate Chantilly Cream

*I*f you are looking for an alternative to pecan pie, this is a great one. Trying to come up with such an alternative a few years ago, I was playing with hazelnuts, milk chocolate, and caramel, which is a great combination, but rather dense. Ice cream as an accompaniment didn't seem to be the answer, and then I thought of chocolate chantilly. This simple combination of melted chocolate and whipping cream adds creaminess on top of the chewy tart, and flavor too, making this very special.

MAKES 6 TO 8 SERVINGS

Special Equipment:
Pastry Bag Fitted with a ⅜-Inch Plain Tip (Such as Ateco #4)

Tart

1½ cups (213 grams) unblanched hazelnuts, toasted and skinned (see page 16)

1½ ounces (42 grams) milk chocolate, finely chopped

1 tablespoon plus 1 teaspoon (28 grams) honey

⅓ cup (67 grams) sugar

1 tablespoon plus 1 teaspoon (26 grams) light corn syrup

Pinch of salt

¼ cup plus 2 tablespoons (87 grams) heavy cream

One 9½-inch tart shell made from Sweet Tart Dough (page 26), prebaked

Chocolate Chantilly

5 ounces (142 grams) milk chocolate, chopped

½ cup plus 2 tablespoons (145 grams) heavy cream, well chilled

Garnish

Milk chocolate curls (see page 21)

1. *Make the tart:* Combine the hazelnuts, milk chocolate, and honey in a medium bowl; set aside.

2. Combine the sugar, corn syrup, and salt in a medium heavy saucepan. Cook over medium-high heat, stirring, until the sugar dissolves. Boil without stirring until the caramel turns a golden amber color, 5 to 7 minutes. Immediately remove the pan from the heat and slowly add the cream. (Stand back—the caramel will bubble up and may splatter a bit.) Stir with a wooden spoon, then set the pan over low heat and cook, stirring, until completely smooth.

3. Pour the hot caramel into the bowl containing the hazelnuts and stir to combine well. Scrape the nut mixture into the tart shell and let it cool. The tart can be made to this point up to 2 days in advance and stored in the refrigerator.

4. *Make the chocolate chantilly:* Up to 3 hours before serving, fill a large saucepan one-third full with water and bring just to a simmer. Place the chocolate in a bowl, set it over the barely simmering water, and heat, stirring constantly, until melted and smooth.

5. In the bowl of an electric mixer, beat the cream on high speed until stiff peaks just begin to form. Gently fold in the warm melted chocolate just until combined.

continued

Hazelnut Tart with Chocolate Chantilly Cream

6. *Garnish the tart:* Fill a pastry bag fitted with a ⅜-inch plain tip with the chocolate chantilly. Pipe the cream in a spiral starting at the outside edge and working toward the center, covering the tart completely. Garnish the center of the tart with milk chocolate curls. Refrigerate until ready to serve. Let the tart stand at room temperature for 20 minutes before serving.

Pierre, cleaning the freezer.

Tarts and Tartlets

Chocolate Tart

8 ounces (227 grams) bittersweet chocolate, finely chopped

⅔ cup (153 grams) heavy cream

½ vanilla bean, split

2 large egg yolks

2 tablespoons (28 grams) unsalted butter, softened and cut into
½-inch cubes

One 9½-inch tart shell made from Sweet Tart Dough (page 26),
prebaked

1. Place the chocolate in a medium bowl and set a sieve over the
bowl. Set aside.

2. Put the cream in a medium saucepan. Scrape the seeds from the
vanilla bean into the pan, add the bean, and bring to a boil. Pour the hot
cream through the sieve onto the chopped chocolate. Allow to stand for
30 seconds to melt the chocolate, then whisk until the chocolate is completely melted and the mixture is smooth. Whisk in the egg yolks and
butter until the butter is melted.

3. Pour the filling into the baked tart shell. Refrigerate until set, at
least 2 hours and up to 24 hours. Bring the tart to room temperature before serving.

I changed the name of this
from its original: Grampa's
Tart. My grandfather used to
make this one for my mother, because she loved chocolate. After
he had baked and cooled it, he
would decorate it with many,
many chocolate cigarettes, a crazy
number of them. You can leave it
plain, but it is fun to decorate
with more chocolate, because this
one was born to be "too much."
The filling is more than a simple
ganache, the classic truffle filling
of cream and chocolate; egg yolks
make this one even richer. You
can accompany this with fresh
raspberries and raspberry sauce,
but it is just fine by itself.

MAKES 6 TO 8 SERVINGS

*Tarts
and
Tartlets*

Warm Chocolate Tart

Warm Chocolate Tart

8 ounces (227 grams) bittersweet chocolate, finely chopped

¾ cup (174 grams) heavy cream

½ cup (121 grams) whole milk

1 large egg, lightly beaten

One 9½-inch tart shell made from Sweet Tart Dough (page 26), prebaked

1. Preheat the oven to 325°F.

2. Place the chopped chocolate in a medium bowl and set aside.

3. Combine the cream and milk in a medium saucepan, and bring to a boil over medium-high heat. Pour the hot cream mixture over the chocolate. Allow to stand for 30 seconds to melt the chocolate, then whisk until the chocolate is completely melted and the mixture is smooth. Allow to cool for 10 minutes.

4. Whisk the egg into the chocolate mixture. Pour the filling into the prebaked tart shell.

5. Bake the tart for 8 to 10 minutes, until the edges of the filling are set; the center will still be soft. Cool the tart on a wire rack for 10 minutes and serve warm.

I have made this amazing tart in every restaurant where I've worked and it never fails to sell out. It is very simple to make. The filling is like a ganache, but the egg adds some air. The rich chocolate creaminess of the tart, the chewiness of the dough, and then the temperature and flavor jolt of vanilla ice cream against the warm tart explain why this is so popular. You can serve it warm or cold, but I recommend warm— make it up to a day ahead of time, then just warm it up again in a low oven.

MAKES 6 TO 8 SERVINGS

Mediterranean Swiss Chard Tart

This is a recipe from the south of France, and it is one my grandfather was proud to serve. I started selling this tart at Payard recently. It was a hit, but it took some effort on the part of my staff. We would offer a free sample of it to customers without telling them what it was, and always get the same response: "Delicious! I've never had anything like it. What is it?" When we told them it was Swiss chard, they flipped out. It was as if we were offering them chicken ice cream! The flavor of Swiss chard is hard to describe. Its very faint spinach-like note is happily sewn into the rum, pastry cream, raisins, and pine nuts. Try it and you'll be surprised—it is an incredible sensation. In France, this is traditionally served cut into squares, with ricotta cheese instead of pastry cream. It is delicious either way.

MAKES 6 SERVINGS

Special Equipment:
14¾ × 4½-Inch Tart Pan with a Removable Bottom

*Tarts
and
Tartlets*

Filling

½ cup (90 grams) raisins

2 tablespoons (28 grams) dark rum, such as Myers's

12 ounces (340 grams) Swiss chard (see Note)

2 cups (500 grams) Pastry Cream (page 28)

2 medium (340 grams) Granny Smith apples, peeled, cored, and cut into ¼-inch dice

⅓ cup (46 grams) pine nuts

Tart

One recipe Sweet Tart Dough (page 26)

Garnish

2 tablespoons (30 grams) Apricot Glaze (page 33)

¼ cup (50 grams) sugar

1. *Soak the raisins:* Combine the raisins and rum in a small airtight container and allow to stand, covered, for at least 8 hours, or overnight.

2. *Make the crust:* On a lightly floured work surface, using a floured rolling pin, roll half of the dough out to a rectangle measuring 17 × 7 inches.

3. Gently lift the rectangle onto a 14¾ × 4½-inch tart pan with a removable bottom. Press the dough into the pan and roll the pin over the top of the pan to remove the excess dough. Prick the bottom of the shell all over with a fork. Follow the directions for partially baking a tart shell on page 26.

4. Once again on a floured surface using a floured rolling pin, roll the remaining dough into a 16 × 6-inch rectangle. Transfer the rectangle to a baking sheet and refrigerate while you make the filling.

5. Preheat the oven to 325°F.

6. *Make the filling:* Using a paring knife, remove and discard the tough center ribs from the Swiss chard leaves. Coarsely chop the chard. Blanch for 3 minutes in a large pot of boiling water; drain well. Squeeze the chard, a small bunch at a time, to remove the excess water and allow it to cool.

7. Drain the raisins. Place the pastry cream in a medium bowl and fold in the diced apples, pine nuts, raisins, and Swiss chard. Transfer the filling to the baked tart shell and spread it evenly with a spatula. Cover the filling with the refrigerated rectangle of unbaked dough, pressing the dough down at the edges to seal it; trim off the excess dough. With a par-

continued

Mediterranean Swiss Chard Tart

ing knife, cut several small slits in the top of the pastry to allow steam to escape.

8. Bake the tart for 45 to 50 minutes, or until the crust is golden brown. Cool the tart on a wire rack.

9. *Garnish the tart:* If necessary, rewarm the apricot glaze over low heat or in the microwave. Brush the top of the tart with the warm glaze and sprinkle with the sugar. Cut the tart into squares to serve. The tart can be made up to 2 days in advance and stored in the refrigerator. Bring to room temperature before serving.

NOTE: Regular Swiss chard has dark green leaves and white stalks. Ruby chard has dark red leaves and red stalks, while the more common red chard has green leaves and reddish stalks. Chard is available throughout the year but is at its peak in the summer months. Store it in a plastic bag in the refrigerator for up to four days.

Asking Executive Chef Philippe Bertineau for a hand.

Apple Financier Tart

Financier Batter

3 tablespoons (43 grams) unsalted butter

½ cup (60 grams) slivered almonds

¼ cup plus 3 tablespoons (50 grams) confectioners' sugar

¼ cup plus 2 tablespoons (54 grams) all-purpose flour

2 tablespoons (15 grams) cornstarch

Pinch of salt

4 large egg whites

2 tablespoons (42 grams) honey

¼ cup (58 grams) heavy cream

1 vanilla bean, split

Apple Filling

10 tablespoons (1¼ sticks) (142 grams) unsalted butter, cut into tablespoons

3 medium (510 grams) Golden Delicious apples, peeled, cored, and cut into ¼-inch dice

½ cup (168 grams) honey

¼ cup (60 grams) Calvados or apple jack

Assembly

One 9½-inch tart shell made from Sweet Tart Dough (page 26), unbaked

Glaze

¼ cup (84 grams) honey

A financier is usually a petit four, made of an almond batter with egg whites and browned butter. This full-size financier was developed by Hervé Poussot, my friend and colleague, to take advantage of the amazing apples that are available in the fall. Consider it a French version of apple pie—but serve it without the ice cream. The moisture of the mix and the texture of the apples with the flavor of the browned butter make this delicious on its own. (We don't decorate with fresh apples, because they turn brown, and then the tart doesn't look nice.) This tart will keep for a week in the refrigerator.

MAKES 6 SERVINGS

1. *Make the financier batter:* Preheat the oven to 350°F.

2. Melt the butter in a small skillet over medium heat. Reduce the heat to medium-low and cook the butter until it begins to brown and has a nutty fragrance, about 3 minutes. Set aside to cool.

3. Put the slivered almonds in a food processor and process until finely ground, about 45 seconds. Transfer the ground almonds to a medium bowl. Sift the confectioners' sugar over the almonds. Add the flour, cornstarch, and salt and gently whisk to combine.

4. Combine the egg whites, honey, cooled browned butter, and cream in another medium bowl. Scrape the seeds from the vanilla bean

continued

Tarts
and
Tartlets

Apple Financier Tart

(reserve the pod for another use) into the bowl and whisk to combine. Add the dry ingredients and whisk just until combined. Set aside.

5. *Make the apple filling:* Melt the butter in a large skillet over medium heat and cook until it is golden brown and fragrant, about 5 minutes. Add the diced apples and honey and cook, stirring occasionally, for 2 minutes, or until the apples are slightly softened. Add the Calvados to the skillet, carefully light it with a match, and cook until the flame dies. Drain the apples in a strainer set over a bowl, reserving ¼ cup of the liquid. Stir the reserved liquid back into the diced apples.

6. Pour the apple mixture into the tart shell and spread it into an even layer. Scrape the financier batter over the apples, covering them completely.

7. Bake the tart for 45 to 50 minutes, until the top is golden brown and a toothpick inserted into the center comes out clean. Place the tart on a wire rack.

8. *Glaze the tart:* Put the honey in a heatproof glass measure and microwave on high for 10 to 15 seconds, until hot. (Or, heat in a small saucepan.) Brush the honey over the top of the hot tart. Cool the tart completely before serving.

Rice Tart

When I was a kid, my favorite treat was a rice custard called Yabo. (You would think with my parents owning a pastry shop, I wouldn't go mad for something from the supermarket in a can, but that's kids for you.) There was a little caramel on the bottom, so you would flip it over and the caramel would pour down over the custard. All the kids loved it. It is such a fond food memory for me that I wanted to share it with others. It is a classic French tart, and the filling is like a flan. It can be served at any time of year along with whatever fruits you have on hand—try citrus fruits in the winter or berries in the summer as an accompaniment.

MAKES 6 TO 8 SERVINGS

Special Equipment:
Instant-Read Thermometer

Tart

⅔ cup (120 grams) raisins

2 tablespoons (28 grams) dark rum, such as Myers's

3¾ cups (907 grams) whole milk

3 tablespoons (37 grams) sugar

2 vanilla beans, split

½ cup (80 grams) long-grain rice

4 large egg yolks

14 tablespoons (1 stick plus 6 tablespoons) (200 grams) unsalted butter, cut into ½-inch cubes and softened

One 9½-inch tart shell made from Sweet Tart Dough (page 26), partially baked

Apple Topping

7 tablespoons (100 grams) unsalted butter, softened

2 medium (340 grams) Granny Smith apples, peeled, cored, and each cut into 8 wedges

½ cup (100 grams) sugar

Glaze

¼ cup (60 grams) Apricot Glaze (page 33)

1. *Make the tart:* Combine the raisins with the rum in an airtight container and allow to soak for at least 8 hours, or overnight.

2. Combine the milk and sugar in a medium saucepan. Scrape the seeds from the vanilla beans into the pan, add the vanilla beans, and bring to a boil over medium-high heat, stirring to dissolve the sugar. Reduce the heat to medium-low, stir in the rice, and simmer for 25 to 30 minutes, until the rice is tender. Reduce the heat to low.

3. Preheat the oven to 325°F.

4. Whisk the egg yolks in a medium bowl until smooth. Whisk in about 1 cup of the hot rice mixture. Whisk the yolk mixture into the rice mixture in the saucepan and cook, stirring constantly with a wooden spoon, until the mixture thickens slightly and reaches 175°F on an instant-read thermometer. (When you draw your finger over the sauce-coated spoon it should leave a path.) Remove the pan from the heat and take the vanilla beans out of the mixture.

5. Drain the raisins. Add the raisins and butter to the rice mixture and stir until the butter is melted. Scrape the hot filling into the tart shell. Smooth the top with a spatula.

6. Bake the tart for 20 to 25 minutes, or until the center is just set. Cool the tart on a wire rack. Leave the oven on and increase the temperature to 350°F.

7. *Make the apple topping:* Generously brush a baking sheet with some of the softened butter. Arrange the apple wedges, cut side up, on the sheet. Brush the apples with the remaining butter and sprinkle with the sugar. Bake for 15 to 20 minutes, until tender. Allow the apples to cool on the pan until just warm to the touch.

8. Arrange the apple wedges on top of the tart in a pinwheel pattern, starting from the edge of the tart and working toward the center.

9. *Glaze the tart:* If necessary, rewarm the apricot glaze over low heat or in the microwave. Using a pastry brush, lightly brush the top of the tart with the glaze. Serve the tart at room temperature or slightly chilled. The tart can be made up to 1 day in advance and stored in the refrigerator.

Samantha, pastry shop manager, and Adrian oversee the quality of the pastries.

Tarts and Tartlets

Tarte Bourdaloue

This is a traditional tart from France, usually made in the wintertime. With the almond cream on the bottom and the flan-like custard on top, this tart remains very moist, and with the pears partially immersed in the custard, it is very pretty too. You can make it a day in advance and store in the refrigerator. It tastes as good, if not better, the day after it is made. You can add Apricot Glaze (page 33) to the top, if you like. Serve with Crème Anglaise (page 31).

MAKES 6 TO 8 SERVINGS

½ cup (105 grams) Almond Cream (page 29)

One 9½-inch tart shell made from Sweet Tart Dough (page 26), unbaked

2 large eggs

3 tablespoons (37 grams) sugar

1 cup plus 1 tablespoon (246 grams) heavy cream

1 teaspoon (4 grams) pure vanilla extract

6 poached (see page 34) or canned pear halves

Garnish

2 tablespoons (11 grams) sliced blanched almonds, toasted (see page 16)

1. Preheat the oven to 325°F.

2. Scrape the almond cream into the tart shell and spread it into an even layer. Bake for 12 to 14 minutes, until the almond layer is puffed but not set; it should not begin to color. Cool the tart on a wire rack. (Leave the oven on.)

3. Whisk together the eggs and sugar in a medium bowl until thickened and pale, about 3 minutes. Whisk in the cream and vanilla extract.

4. Arrange the pear halves, cut side down and with the stem ends toward the center, on the almond layer. Pour the custard mixture over the pears.

5. Bake for 45 to 50 minutes, until the custard is set and the pastry is golden brown. Cool the tart completely on a wire rack. Sprinkle the tart with the almonds before serving.

Tarte Bourdaloue

Banana Tartlets

This is a simplified version of a recipe I created in Paris, and it really is a young pastry chef's attempt to reinvent the tart: white chocolate mousse, rum-sautéed bananas, and crushed cashews in phyllo dough. It makes perfect sense. The cashews bring out the flavor of the banana, the rum is a classic companion to banana, and the white chocolate mousse is a mellow canvas that highlights the other flavors. Although many people pair banana and caramel, I don't. I love caramel, but it is sweet, and bananas are already sweet enough. I like to cut that sweetness here, with the salted cashews. Serve with vanilla ice cream.

MAKES 4 SERVINGS

Special Equipment:
4-Inch Biscuit Cutter;
Four 2-Inch-High 4-Inch
Ring Molds

White Chocolate Mousse

¾ cup (174 grams) heavy cream

9 ounces (255 grams) white chocolate, chopped

Phyllo Rounds

¾ cup (95 grams) salted cashews

¼ cup (49 grams) Clarified Butter (page 38)

4 sheets (12 × 17 inches) phyllo dough, thawed if frozen

3 tablespoons (21 grams) confectioners' sugar, sifted

Banana Rum Filling

2 tablespoons (28 grams) unsalted butter

1 tablespoon (12 grams) sugar

2 medium bananas, peeled and cut into ½-inch slices

¼ cup (55 grams) dark rum, such as Myers's

Garnish

4 scoops Vanilla Ice Cream (page 177)

1. *Make the white chocolate mousse:* Line the bottom of a 9-inch square baking pan with parchment paper. In an electric mixer fitted with the whisk attachment, whip the cream to soft peaks. Cover and refrigerate.

2. Fill a medium saucepan one-third full with water and bring just to a low simmer. Place the white chocolate in a medium bowl, set it over the barely simmering water, and stir until melted. Using a large rubber spatula, gently fold the melted chocolate into the whipped cream. Scrape the mousse into the prepared baking pan, spreading it in an even layer. Freeze until hard, at least 3 hours.

3. *Make the phyllo rounds:* Place the cashews in a heavy-duty resealable bag. With a hammer or heavy pan, gently crush the cashews into small pieces. Set aside.

4. Preheat the oven to 375°F. Line a baking sheet with parchment paper and brush with some of the clarified butter.

5. Place 1 phyllo sheet on a large piece of parchment paper on a work surface. Brush the phyllo with clarified butter and sprinkle with the crushed cashews. Lay another phyllo sheet over the top. Place a baking sheet on top of the phyllo sheets, place a heavy pot or other weight on top and press down to flatten the phyllo sheets. Remove the pot and baking sheet. Brush the phyllo sheet with clarified butter and sprinkle with half of the confectioners' sugar. Cover with a third phyllo sheet, brush with butter, and sprinkle with the remaining confectioners' sugar. Top with the fourth phyllo sheet and flatten again using the baking sheet and pot. With a 4-inch round cutter, cut out 8 rounds from the phyllo layers.

6. Place four 4 × 2-inch-high ring molds on a baking sheet and fit one phyllo round in each mold. Bake the phyllo shells for 6 to 8 minutes, or until golden brown. Set the lined rings and the rounds on a wire rack to cool completely.

7. *Make the banana rum filling:* Melt the butter in a large skillet over medium-high heat. Stir in the sugar and cook for 1 minute, until the sugar is dissolved. Add the bananas and rum and cook for another minute, stirring to coat the bananas. Remove the pan from the heat and set aside.

8. *Assemble the dessert:* Using the 4-inch round cutter, cut out four rounds from the white chocolate mousse. Place one round in each ring mold. Top with the 4-inch phyllo rounds. Spoon the banana filling over the phyllo, dividing it evenly among the ring molds and pressing down lightly with the spoon.

9. Place each ring mold on a dessert plate and remove the mold by lifting it up while you press down on the banana layer. Top each tartlet with a scoop of vanilla ice cream. The tarts can be made up to 1 day in advance and stored, well covered, in the refrigerator. Let stand at room temperature for 30 minutes before serving.

Chocolate Ganache Tartlets

This is a perfect dessert to serve at the end of a rich meal: The tartlets are small, but rich and chocolaty, and the touch of cinnamon in the filling makes these a perfect match for coffee. This is not a true ganache—we use milk rather than cream, and I add some butter to the ganache, for richness and some creaminess.

MAKES 30 TARTLETS

Special Equipment:
Thirty 2-Inch Tartlet Pans, Pastry Bag Fitted with a ¼-Inch Star Tip (Such as Ateco #2)

14 ounces (397 grams) bittersweet chocolate, chopped (see Note)

9 tablespoons (128 grams) unsalted butter, cut into tablespoons, softened

1 cup plus 2 tablespoons (272 grams) whole milk

1 cinnamon stick

1 recipe Sweet Tart Dough (page 26)

30 hazelnuts, toasted and skinned (see page 16)

1. Place the chocolate in a large bowl. Place the softened butter on top of the chocolate. Set a sieve over the bowl.

2. Bring the milk and cinnamon stick to a boil in a medium saucepan. Immediately pour the milk through the sieve onto the chocolate and butter. Whisk gently until the chocolate and butter are melted and the ganache is smooth. Set aside to cool.

3. Preheat the oven to 350°F. Arrange thirty 2-inch round tartlet pans close together on a baking sheet.

4. On a lightly floured surface, roll out the dough to a ¹⁄₁₆-inch thickness. Roll the dough up onto the rolling pin and unroll it over the tartlet pans. Press the dough into the molds with your fingers. Roll the pin over the molds, pressing down until you see the outline of the molds through the dough. Remove the excess dough from between the molds.

5. Bake the tartlet shells for 6 to 8 minutes, until golden brown. Cool the shells in their pans on a wire rack.

6. When the tartlet shells are cool, remove them from the molds. Fill a pastry bag fitted with a ¼-inch star tip with the cooled ganache. Pipe a generous rosette of the ganache into each tartlet shell and top each with a hazelnut. Refrigerate the tarts for up to 1 day if not serving immediately. Bring to room temperature before serving.

NOTE: If possible, use a chocolate with a 60 to 65 percent cocoa content. (These percentages are listed on the packages of European chocolate, such as Callebaut.)

Soufflés

The French word *soufflé* means to blow or to breathe, but I fear that for some people the word represents everything that is intimidating and fussy in French food. Actually, a warm soufflé is quite simple to prepare. The flavor is sublime, and it's extremely gratifying to serve a soufflé because it always impresses your friends.

A soufflé is simply an egg-based custard with a lot of air whipped into the whites; as it is baked in its special mold, the outside forms a crust, while the air and steam trapped inside causes it to rise. When you part the top of a warm soufflé with your spoon, you will see the center is a little bit loose. Don't worry, that's the way it is supposed to be. While you start to eat the top, which is baked, the mold remains warm, so when you stir the center of the soufflé together with the outer part, which is slightly cooked, you create the right consistency.

All of these soufflés are presented as individual soufflés because they bake more evenly than a large soufflé in a large dish. They are easier to serve properly, because you don't waste time doling out portions. They look prettier and more contemporary, and they allow you to pour sauce into the center of each serving.

Let me show you a foolproof way to make a warm soufflé—or rather, let my grandfather show you, because he was a specialist in soufflés, and his were incredible. For a fruit soufflé, most restaurant kitchens will add the flavoring agent to a pastry cream, which is made with egg yolks, then add the egg whites. My grandfather taught me that what stabilizes a soufflé is the egg yolks. The yolks are like the pastry cream in these soufflés. We mix the flavoring elements and then add the egg yolks, using a blender. This emulsifies and stabilizes the custard, and it always works.

I have also included a number of frozen soufflés. Creamy and rich, like ice cream, these should be made the day before they are to be served. You can make them as much as a week in advance. For these frozen soufflés, you use a collar—a strip of foil that extends above the top of the ramekin—so that you can overfill the mold. Once the soufflé is frozen, you remove the collar, and it looks as if the soufflé has risen above the rim of the ramekin. That "rise" is what entitles it to be called a soufflé.

Warm Apricot Soufflé

This soufflé is delicious served with raspberries or a raspberry sauce.

MAKES 6 SERVINGS

Special Equipment:
Six 6-Ounce Ramekins;
Pastry Bag Fitted with a ½-Inch
Plain Tip (Such as Ateco #6)

One 15¼-ounce can apricot halves, drained

2 large eggs, separated, at room temperature

½ cup (100 grams) sugar

1 tablespoon (25 grams) peach schnapps or apricot liqueur

3 large egg whites, at room temperature

1 tablespoon (16 grams) fresh lemon juice

1. Preheat the oven to 350°F. Generously brush the insides of six 6-ounce ramekins with butter. Chill the ramekins in the freezer for 15 minutes. Brush them again with butter and coat them with sugar, tapping out the excess. Reserve the ramekins in the refrigerator.

2. Purée the apricots in a blender until smooth. Add the egg yolks, 2 tablespoons (25 grams) of the sugar, and the peach schnapps and blend on medium speed for 2 minutes, or until the mixture is smooth and thickened. Transfer the mixture to a medium bowl.

3. In the clean dry bowl of an electric mixer, with the whisk attachment, beat the 5 egg whites on low speed until foamy. Add the lemon juice and beat on medium speed until soft peaks form. Gradually beat in the remaining ¼ cup plus 2 tablespoons (75 grams) sugar, then beat on high speed until stiff peaks form. Using a large rubber spatula, fold one scoop of the meringue into the apricot mixture, then gently fold in the remaining meringue.

4. Fill a pastry bag fitted with a ½-inch plain tip with the soufflé mixture. Pipe the mixture into the ramekins, filling them three-quarters full. Run your thumb around the inside edge of each ramekin, wiping off the butter and sugar from the rim.

5. Place the ramekins on a baking sheet and bake the soufflés for 10 to 12 minutes, until puffed and golden. Serve immediately.

Warm Pear Soufflé

One 15¼-ounce can pear halves, drained and cut into chunks

2 large eggs, separated, at room temperature

½ cup (100 grams) sugar

1 tablespoon (12 grams) Poire Williams liqueur

3 large egg whites, at room temperature

2 tablespoons (31 grams) fresh lemon juice

1. Preheat the oven to 350°F. Generously brush the insides of six 6-ounce ramekins with butter. Chill the ramekins in the freezer for 15 minutes. Brush them again with butter and coat them with sugar, tapping out the excess. Reserve the ramekins in the refrigerator.

2. Purée the pears in a blender until smooth. Add the egg yolks, 2 tablespoons (25 grams) of the sugar, and the liqueur and blend on medium speed for 2 minutes, or until the mixture is smooth and emulsified. Transfer the mixture to a medium bowl.

3. In the clean dry bowl of an electric mixer, with the whisk attachment, beat the 5 egg whites on low speed until foamy. Add the lemon juice and beat on medium speed until soft peaks form. Gradually beat in the remaining ¼ cup plus 2 tablespoons (75 grams) sugar, then beat at high speed until stiff peaks form. Using a large rubber spatula, fold one scoop of the meringue into the pear mixture, then gently fold in the remaining meringue.

4. Fill a pastry bag fitted with a ½-inch plain tip with the soufflé mixture. Pipe the mixture into the ramekins, filling them three-quarters full. Run your thumb around the inside edge of each ramekin, wiping off the butter and sugar from the rim.

5. Place the ramekins on a baking sheet and bake the soufflés for 10 to 12 minutes, until puffed and golden. Serve immediately.

Serve this with Strawberry Marmalade (page 33) for an extraordinary combination of flavor. I suggest that you place the marmalade—or any sauce or ice cream accompanying these soufflés—in serving dishes in the center of the table. Your guests can then spoon as much as they like in the center of the soufflé. Sublime.

MAKES 6 SERVINGS

Special Equipment:
Six 6-Ounce Ramekins;
Pastry Bag Fitted with a ½-Inch
Plain Tip (Such as Ateco #6)

Soufflés

Warm Chocolate Soufflé

Not along ago, I tried the chocolate soufflé at a famous New York restaurant. It was utterly tasteless, and I am being charitable when I say that the chef must have forgotten to put the chocolate in. If you have ever been disappointed as I was, it was probably because it is common for chocolate soufflés served in restaurants to be made with cocoa powder, not chocolate. And if that has been your experience, you have not yet had a real chocolate soufflé. Because it is made with a ganache, don't expect this one to rise as much as a fruit soufflé. Serve with Pistachio Ice Cream (page 181) or Vanilla Ice Cream (page 177).

MAKES 8 SERVINGS

Special Equipment:
Eight 6-Ounce Ramekins; Pastry Bag Fitted with a ½-Inch Plain Tip (Such as Ateco #6)

7 ounces (198 grams) bittersweet chocolate, chopped

3 tablespoons (43 grams) unsalted butter, cut into ½-inch cubes

1 tablespoon (15 grams) crème fraîche, optional

4 large eggs, separated, at room temperature

3 large egg whites, at room temperature

½ teaspoon (1.5 grams) cream of tartar

⅓ cup (66 grams) sugar

1. Generously brush the insides of eight 6-ounce ramekins with butter. Chill the ramekins in the freezer for 15 minutes. Brush them again with butter and coat them with sugar, tapping out the excess. Reserve the ramekins in the refrigerator.

2. Fill a medium saucepan one-third full with water and bring to a simmer. Place the chocolate and butter in a medium bowl, set it over the simmering water, and melt the chocolate and butter, stirring occasionally until completely smooth. Whisk in the crème fraîche, if using. Set the chocolate mixture aside to cool.

3. Preheat the oven to 350°F. Whisk the yolks into the cooled chocolate until smooth.

4. In the clean dry bowl of an electric mixer, with the whisk attachment, beat the 7 egg whites on low speed until foamy. Add the cream of tartar and beat on medium speed until they form soft peaks. Gradually add the sugar and mix on high speed until stiff peaks form. Using a large rubber spatula, fold a scoop of the beaten whites into the chocolate mixture, then gently fold in the remaining whites.

5. Fill a pastry bag fitted with a ½-inch plain tip with the soufflé mixture. Pipe the mixture into the ramekins, filling them three-quarters full. Run your thumb around the inside edge of each ramekin, wiping off the butter and sugar from the rim.

6. Place the ramekins on a baking sheet and bake the soufflés for 11 to 13 minutes, until puffed. Serve immediately.

Warm Praline Soufflé

1 cup (250 grams) Pastry Cream (page 28)

4 large eggs, separated, at room temperature

½ cup (150 grams) Praline Paste (page 36, or see Sources, page 225)

8 large egg whites, at room temperature

1 teaspoon (3 grams) cream of tartar

¼ cup (50 grams) sugar

⅓ cup (28 grams) blanched sliced almonds

1. Preheat the oven to 350°F. Generously brush the insides of nine 6-ounce ramekins with butter. Chill the ramekins in the freezer for 15 minutes. Brush them again with butter and coat with sugar, tapping out the excess. Reserve the ramekins in the refrigerator.

2. Place the pastry cream in a large bowl and whisk in the egg yolks until smooth. Whisk in the praline paste; set aside.

3. In the clean dry bowl of an electric mixer, with the whisk attachment, beat the 12 egg whites on low speed until they are foamy. Add the cream of tartar and beat on medium speed until soft peaks form. Gradually beat in the sugar, then beat at high speed until stiff peaks form. Using a large rubber spatula, fold one scoop of the beaten whites into the pastry cream mixture, then gently fold in the remaining whites.

4. Fill a pastry bag fitted with a ½-inch plain tip with the soufflé mixture. Pipe the mixture into the ramekins, filling them three-quarters full. Run your thumb around the inside edge of each ramekin, wiping off the butter and sugar from the rim. Sprinkle the soufflés with the almonds.

5. Place the soufflés on a baking sheet and bake for 10 to 12 minutes, until puffed and golden. Serve immediately.

*W*armth brings out the flavor of nuts, and when they are sweetened, as in praline paste, the taste is memorable. I've always enjoyed drinking coffee with nutty desserts, so I recommend that you serve this with coffee, and perhaps Vanilla Ice Cream (page 177) too, if you like. The pastry cream can be made up to five days in advance and stored, well covered, in the refrigerator.

MAKES 9 SERVINGS

Special Equipment:
Nine 6-Ounce Ramekins;
Pastry Bag Fitted with a ½-Inch
Plain Tip (Such as Ateco #6)

Soufflés

Warm Harlequin Soufflé

When I was working in France, people were crazy for anything "harlequin." Harlequin is a figure in classic French comedy and pantomime who dresses in a multicolored costume; the word *harlequin* has thus come to denote anything that is multicolored. For this soufflé, strips of cardboard are arranged in the molds to create four separate compartments, into which you pipe alternate soufflé bases. This one is pistachio and vanilla, but I also recommend chocolate and praline. You can mix and match the soufflé mixtures any way you like as long as the cooking times indicated in the two recipes are the same. You cannot mix chocolate with pear, for example, because the chocolate soufflés cook for slightly longer—but this still leaves many possibilities. As in the Warm Praline Soufflé (page 163), the pastry cream can be made up to five days in advance and stored, well covered, in the refrigerator.

MAKE 9 SERVINGS

Special Equipment:
Nine 6-Ounce Ramekins;
Two Pastry Bags Fitted with ½-Inch
Plain Tips (Such as Ateco #6)

1 cup (250 grams) Pastry Cream (page 28)

4 large eggs, separated, at room temperature

½ cup (100 grams) Pistachio Paste (page 37, or see Sources, page 225)

8 large egg whites, at room temperature

1 teaspoon (3 grams) cream of tartar

¼ cup (50 grams) sugar

1. Using lightweight cardboard (such as manila file folders), cut out eighteen 3⅝-inch squares (the squares should fit, standing upright, snugly but without buckling, in the ramekins). Make a 1½-inch cut from the middle of one edge of each square to the middle of the square. Form nine three-dimensional crosses out of the squares by joining pairs of the squares at the slits. Set the crosses aside.

2. Preheat the oven to 350°F. Generously brush the insides of nine 6-ounce ramekins with butter. Chill the ramekins in the freezer for 15 minutes. Brush them again with butter and coat with sugar, tapping out the excess. Place a cardboard cross in each ramekin to partition it into four compartments. Reserve the ramekins in the refrigerator.

3. Place the pastry cream in a medium bowl and whisk in the egg yolks. Transfer half of the pastry cream to another medium bowl and whisk in the pistachio paste.

4. In the clean dry bowl of an electric mixer, with the whisk attachment, beat the 12 egg whites on low speed until foamy. Add the cream of tartar and beat on medium speed until soft peaks form. Gradually beat in the sugar, then beat at high speed until stiff peaks form.

5. Transfer half of the whites to a medium bowl. Using a rubber spatula, fold one scoop of these whites into the vanilla pastry cream, then gently fold in the remaining whites in the bowl. Repeat with the remaining whites and the pistachio pastry cream.

6. Fill a pastry bag fitted with a ½-inch plain tip with the vanilla soufflé mixture. Fill three-quarters of two opposite quarters of each ramekin with this mixture. Fill a second pastry bag fitted with a ½-inch plain tip with the pistachio mixture. Fill the remaining quarters of each ramekin three-quarters full with the pistachio mixture. Slowly lift out the cardboard partitions. Run your thumb around the inside edge of each ramekin, wiping off the butter and sugar from the rim.

7. Place the ramekins on a baking sheet and bake the soufflés for 10 to 12 minutes, until puffed and golden. Serve immediately.

Frozen Apricot Soufflé

12 ounces (350 grams) canned apricot halves (about 14 halves)
(see Note)

2 cups (464 grams) heavy cream

3 large eggs, separated, at room temperature

5 large egg yolks, at room temperature

1 cup (200 grams) sugar

2½ tablespoons (50 grams) light corn syrup

*A*pricot is one of those un-canny flavors that benefits from being either warmed or chilled. Serve this, like the Warm Apricot Soufflé (page 160), with raspberries or a raspberry sauce.

MAKES 8 SERVINGS

Special Equipment:
Eight 4-Ounce Ramekins;
Candy Thermometer;
Pastry Bag Fitted with a ½-Inch
|Plain Tip (Such as Ateco #6)

1. Cut 8 strips of aluminum foil measuring 12 × 5 inches. Fold the strips lengthwise in half. Wrap one strip around each of eight 4-ounce ramekins—the collars should extend about 1 inch above the rims of the ramekins. Secure the collars with tape.

2. Place the apricots in a blender or food processor and purée until smooth. Transfer the purée to a small bowl, cover, and refrigerate until ready to use.

3. In the clean bowl of the electric mixer, with the whisk attachment, beat the heavy cream on high speed to soft peaks. Refrigerate until ready to use.

4. Place the 8 egg yolks in the bowl of an electric mixer fitted with the whisk attachment and beat on medium speed. Meanwhile, place ½ cup (100 grams) of the sugar, the corn syrup, and 2 tablespoons (29 grams) water in a small heavy saucepan and cook over medium heat, stirring until the sugar dissolves. Increase the heat to high and cook without stirring until a candy thermometer registers 243°F. Immediately remove the pan from the heat, turn the mixer speed to low, and pour the syrup over the egg yolks, being careful to avoid the beater. Increase the speed to medium-high and beat until the yolks have doubled in volume and are almost cool, about 5 minutes. Transfer to a large bowl.

5. In a clean dry mixer bowl, with the clean dry whisk attachment, beat the egg whites on medium speed. Meanwhile, place the remaining ½ cup (100 grams) sugar and 2 tablespoons (29 grams) water in a small saucepan and heat over medium-high heat, stirring, until the sugar dissolves. Wash down the sides of the pan with a wet pastry brush. Cook without stirring until the mixture reaches 243°F on a candy thermometer. Immediately remove from the heat and, with the mixer on, pour the hot syrup over the whites, being careful to avoid the beater. Increase the speed to medium-high and beat until the whites form stiff peaks and are almost cool.

continued

Soufflés

Frozen Apricot Soufflé

6. Using a large rubber spatula, fold the apricot purée into the beaten egg yolks. Fold the beaten egg whites into the whipped cream. Fold this mixture into the beaten egg yolks.

7. Fill a large pastry bag fitted with a ½-inch plain tip with the soufflé mixture. Pipe the mixture into the prepared ramekins, filling them to the top of the collars. (Or spoon the mixture into the ramekins.) Freeze the soufflés for at least 6 hours, or overnight. Remove the collars just before serving.

NOTE: This is the equivalent of a little more than a 15¼-ounce can of pitted apricot halves in syrup, drained. You can use the leftover apricots to garnish the soufflés, or purée them and serve the purée alongside the soufflés.

Frozen Cantaloupe-Strawberry Soufflé

*C*antaloupe and strawberry is a bracing flavor combination, and it works wonderfully in a frozen dessert. Serve with fresh strawberries or Strawberry Marmalade (page 33).

MAKES 8 SERVINGS

Special Equipment:
Eight 4-Ounce Ramekins;
Candy Thermometer;
Pastry Bag Fitted with a ½-Inch
Plain Tip (Such as Ateco #6)

½ ripe cantaloupe, peeled, seeded, and cut into chunks

½ pint (113 grams) strawberries, hulled and cut into quarters

3 large eggs, separated, at room temperature

5 large egg yolks, at room temperature

1 cup (200 grams) sugar

2½ tablespoons (50 grams) light corn syrup

2 cups (464 grams) heavy cream

1. Cut 8 strips of aluminum foil measuring 12 × 5 inches. Fold the strips lengthwise in half. Wrap one strip around each of eight 4-ounce ramekins—the collars should extend about 1 inch above the rims of the ramekins. Secure the collars with tape.

2. Combine the cantaloupe chunks and strawberries in a food processor or blender and process until smooth. Strain the purée through a fine-mesh sieve. You will need 1⅓ cups (345 grams) of purée. Cover the purée and refrigerate.

3. Place the 8 egg yolks in the bowl of an electric mixer fitted with the whisk attachment and beat on medium speed. Meanwhile, place ½ cup (100 grams) of the sugar, the corn syrup, and 2 tablespoons (29 grams) water in a small heavy saucepan and cook over medium heat, stirring, until the sugar is dissolved. Increase the heat to high and cook without stirring until a candy thermometer registers 243°F. Immediately remove the pan from the heat, turn the mixer speed to low, and pour the syrup over the egg yolks, being careful to avoid the beater. Increase the speed to medium-high and beat until the yolks have doubled in volume and are almost cool, about 5 minutes. Transfer to a large bowl.

4. In the clean bowl of the electric mixer, with the whisk attachment, beat the heavy cream on high speed to soft peaks. Refrigerate until ready to use.

5. In a clean dry mixer bowl, with the clean dry whisk attachment, beat the egg whites on medium-low speed. Meanwhile, place the remaining ½ cup (100 grams) sugar and 2 tablespoons (29 grams) water in a small saucepan and cook over medium heat, stirring to dissolve the sugar. Increase the heat to high and cook without stirring until the mixture reaches 243°F on a candy thermometer. Immediately remove from the heat and, with the mixer on, pour the hot syrup over the whites, being careful to avoid the beater. Increase the speed to medium-high and beat until the whites form stiff peaks and are almost cool, about 5 minutes.

6. Stir the cantaloupe-strawberry purée into the egg yolk mixture. Using a large rubber spatula, fold a scoop of the beaten egg whites into the whipped cream. Gently fold in the remaining whites. Fold a scoop of this mixture into the beaten egg yolks; fold in the remaining mixture.

7. Fill a large pastry bag fitted with a ½-inch plain tip with the soufflé mixture. Pipe the mixture into the prepared ramekins, filling them to the top of the collars. (Or spoon in the soufflé mixture.) Freeze the soufflés for at least 6 hours, or overnight. Remove the collars just before serving.

Hervé Poussot, pastry chef, and I work on a new pastry.

Soufflés

Frozen Coconut Soufflé

y wife has always told me that she could cook but she couldn't bake or make desserts; the precision required for baking and dessert making is too stressful, she said. But knowing how much I love coconut, she made this for me and some friends, and it was a stress-free success. These can be served with Strawberry Marmalade (page 33). The cold soufflé and the room-temperature marmalade bring out the best in each other.

MAKES 8 SERVINGS

Special Equipment:
Eight 4-Ounce Ramekins;
Candy Thermometer;
Large Pastry Bag Fitted with
a ½-Inch Plain Tip (Such
as Ateco #6)

3 large eggs, separated, at room temperature

5 large egg yolks, at room temperature

1 cup (200 grams) sugar

2½ tablespoons (50 grams) light corn syrup

2 cups (464 grams) heavy cream

3 tablespoons (50 grams) coconut liqueur, such as Malibu

⅓ cup (26 grams) unsweetened dried shredded coconut

1. Cut 8 strips of aluminum foil measuring 12 × 5 inches. Fold the strips lengthwise in half. Wrap one strip around each of eight 4-ounce ramekins—the collars should extend about 1 inch above the rim of the ramekins. Secure the collars with tape.

2. Place the 8 egg yolks in the bowl of an electric mixer fitted with the whisk attachment and beat on medium speed. Place ½ cup (100 grams) of the sugar, the corn syrup, and 2 tablespoons (29 grams) water in a saucepan and cook over medium heat, stirring, until the sugar is dissolved. Increase the heat to high and cook without stirring until a candy thermometer registers 243°F. Remove the pan from the heat, turn the mixer speed to low, and pour the syrup over the egg yolks, being careful to avoid the beater. Increase the speed to medium-high and beat until the yolks have doubled in volume and are almost cool. Transfer to a large bowl.

4. In the clean bowl of the electric mixer, with the whisk attachment, beat the heavy cream and coconut liqueur on high speed to soft peaks. Refrigerate until ready to use.

5. In a clean dry mixer bowl, with the clean dry whisk attachment, beat the egg whites on low speed. Meanwhile, place the remaining ½ cup (100 grams) sugar and 2 tablespoons (29 grams) water in a small saucepan and heat over medium-high heat, stirring, until the sugar is dissolved. Wash down the sides of the pan with a wet pastry brush. Cook without stirring until the mixture reaches 243°F on a candy thermometer. Immediately remove from the heat and, with the mixer on, pour the hot syrup over the whites, being careful to avoid the beater. Increase the speed to medium-high and beat until the whites form stiff peaks and are almost cool.

6. Using a large rubber spatula, fold the coconut into the egg yolk mixture. Fold a scoop of the beaten egg whites into the whipped cream, then fold in the remaining whites. Fold a scoop of this mixture into the beaten egg yolks; fold in the remaining mixture.

7. Fill a pastry bag fitted with a ½-inch plain tip with the soufflé mixture. Pipe the soufflé mixture into the ramekins to fill. Freeze the soufflés for at least 6 hours, or overnight. Remove the collars before serving.

Frozen Coconut Soufflé

Frozen Nougat Soufflé

If you think about how important nougat is to the flavor of some of your favorite candy bars, you will appreciate how delicious this soufflé is. It has more texture than the other soufflés in this chapter. The toasted almonds add some crunch to every bite, and the raisins, which should be soaked in the rum for at least eight hours, add some flavor spike as well. If you don't care for raisins, dried apricots work well too. This can be served with raspberry sauce and fresh raspberries.

MAKES 8 SERVINGS

Special Equipment:
Eight 4-Ounce Ramekins;
Candy Thermometer

½ cup (90 grams) raisins

¼ cup plus 2 tablespoons (82 grams) dark rum, such as Myers's

5 cups (425 grams) blanched sliced almonds

¼ cup (82 grams) light corn syrup

1 tablespoon plus 1 teaspoon (10 grams) confectioners' sugar

10 large egg whites, at room temperature

1 teaspoon (3 grams) cream of tartar

¾ cup (150 grams) granulated sugar

1 tablespoon plus 1 teaspoon (28 grams) honey

2½ cups (580 grams) heavy cream

1. Combine the raisins and rum in a small airtight container, and let stand for at least 8 hours, or overnight.

2. Preheat the oven to 325°F. Line a baking sheet with parchment paper.

3. Place the almonds and corn syrup in a medium bowl and toss until the almonds are coated. Spread the almonds on the baking sheet in an even layer. Sift the confectioners' sugar through a fine-mesh sieve over the nuts. Bake for 15 to 18 minutes, until light brown. Remove the nuts from the oven and allow to cool completely on the baking sheet.

4. Cut 8 strips of aluminum foil measuring 12 × 5 inches. Fold the strips lengthwise in half. Wrap one strip around each of eight 4-ounce ramekins—the collars should extend about 1 inch above the rims of the ramekins. Secure the collars with tape.

5. Transfer the cooled almonds to a medium bowl and stir with a wooden spoon to break up the large nut clusters; set aside. Drain the raisins and set aside.

6. In the clean dry bowl of an electric mixer fitted with the whisk attachment, beat the egg whites on medium-low speed until foamy. Beat in the cream of tartar. Meanwhile, combine the granulated sugar, 1 tablespoon (15 grams) water, and the honey in a small saucepan and cook over high heat, stirring, until the sugar is dissolved. Cook without stirring until the mixture reaches 243°F on a candy thermometer. Immediately remove from the heat and, with the mixer on, pour the hot syrup over the whites, being careful to avoid the beater. Increase the speed to medium-high and beat until the whites form stiff peaks and are almost cool.

7. In another mixer bowl, with the whisk attachment, beat the heavy cream on high speed to soft peaks.

8. Using a large rubber spatula, fold a scoop of the beaten egg whites into the whipped cream. Gently fold in the remaining whites, then fold in the raisins and almonds.

9. Spoon the soufflé mixture into the ramekins, filling them to the top of the collars. Freeze the soufflés for at least 8 hours, or overnight. Remove the collars just before serving.

Frozen Chocolate Soufflé

My friend's grandmother used to make this soufflé, and whenever word got around that she was busy in the kitchen, every kid within miles was at her door. This is delicious served with chopped pistachios sprinkled on top or with whipped cream.

MAKES 6 SERVINGS

Special Equipment:
Six 4-Ounce Ramekins;
Instant-Read Thermometer

5 ounces (142 grams) bittersweet chocolate, chopped

2 cups (464 grams) heavy cream

¾ cup (181 grams) whole milk

5 large egg yolks

¾ cup (150 grams) sugar

1. Cut 6 strips of aluminum foil measuring 12 × 5 inches. Fold the strips lengthwise in half. Wrap 1 strip around each of six 4-ounce ramekins—the collars should extend about 1 inch above the rims of the ramekins. Secure the collars with tape.

2. Fill a large saucepan one-third full with water and bring to a simmer. Place the chocolate and ⅔ cup (154 grams) of the heavy cream in a bowl, set over the simmering water, and heat, stirring frequently, until the chocolate is completely melted and the mixture is smooth. Set the chocolate mixture aside to cool.

3. Half-fill a large bowl with cold water. Add two large handfuls of ice cubes and set this ice bath aside.

4. Bring the milk to a boil in a medium saucepan over medium-high heat. Remove the pan from the heat and set aside.

5. Whisk the egg yolks and sugar in a medium bowl until thickened and pale, about 3 minutes. Whisk half of the hot milk into the yolks. Pour this mixture into the remaining milk in the saucepan and cook over medium heat, stirring constantly with a wooden spoon, until the mixture thickens and reaches 175°F on an instant-read thermometer. Remove the pan from the heat and strain through a fine-mesh sieve into a medium bowl. Place the bowl in the larger bowl of ice water (add another handful of ice, if necessary) and stir occasionally until cold.

6. In the bowl of an electric mixer fitted with the whisk attachment, beat the remaining 1⅓ cups (310 grams) heavy cream on high speed to soft peaks.

7. Whisk the egg yolk mixture into the cooled chocolate mixture. Using a large rubber spatula, fold in a scoop of the whipped cream. Gently fold in the remaining cream.

8. Spoon the chocolate mixture into the prepared ramekins, filling them to the top of the collars. Freeze the soufflés for at least 6 hours, or overnight. Remove the collars just before serving.

Ice Creams, Sorbets, and Granités

*P*eople rave about their computers and cell phones, but to me the most exciting invention is the home ice cream machine. You can buy a good ice cream machine for as little as $35 and make any ice cream, sorbet, or granité you like—and it's easy.

Everyone has his or her own idea of how dense or how airy ice cream should be. My ice creams are rich, creamy, and delicious. Most of them are made with half-and-half and, in the French tradition, I like to use a generous amount of egg yolks.

Here I offer some of my favorite flavors—coconut and praline, for example; these can stand alone, but they also make wonderful accompaniments to so many tarts and pies and other desserts. I also present some classics, but with my own twist—caramel candy in caramel ice cream, chocolate ice cream with a touch of honey. And there are some frozen treats that will intrigue you—can you really resist Pink Champagne and Raspberry Granité?

These frozen desserts can also be paired with one another. Granité spooned over ice cream is delightful. Serve small scoops of various ice creams and sorbets together. I also recommend many of these as accompaniments to other desserts in this book.

Chocolate Sorbet, Citrus Sorbet, Lemon Ice Cream, Mango Sorbet, Pistachio-Praline Ice Cream, Strawberry Sorbet

Vanilla Ice Cream

2 cups (464 grams) half-and-half

1 vanilla bean, split

6 large egg yolks

⅔ cup (134 grams) sugar

1. Place the half-and-half in a saucepan, scrape the seeds from the vanilla bean into the pan, and add the pod. Bring to a boil. Remove the pan from the heat, cover, and allow to infuse for 10 minutes.

2. Half-fill a large bowl with cold water and add 2 large handfuls of ice cubes; set aside.

3. Place the egg yolks and sugar in a medium bowl and whisk together until thickened and pale, about 3 minutes. Continuing to whisk, drizzle in half of the warm half-and-half. Return this mixture to the pan and whisk to combine. Place the pan over medium heat and cook, stirring constantly with a wooden spoon, until the mixture thickens slightly and reaches 175°F on an instant-read thermometer (a path will remain when you draw your finger across the sauce-coated spoon). This should take about 4 minutes; do not allow the mixture to boil. Remove the pan from the heat and immediately strain the custard through a fine-mesh sieve into a medium bowl.

4. Set the bowl of custard into the bowl of ice water and stir occasionally until it is cold. (At this point, the custard can be stored, covered, in the refrigerator for up to 1 day before freezing.)

5. Pour the chilled custard into an ice cream maker and freeze according to the manufacturer's instructions. Serve immediately or pack into an airtight container and store in the freezer for 1 week.

PRUNE-ARMAGNAC ICE CREAM

For a simple but sophisticated variation, add some macerated prunes and Armagnac to the recipe for vanilla ice cream. A small scoop with pound cake makes an unusual dessert, sure to tantalize your guests.

Combine ¾ cup (166 grams) Armagnac or cognac with 5 ounces (142 grams) pitted prunes in a medium saucepan. Bring to a boil, reduce the heat to low, partially cover, and simmer until the prunes are tender but not mushy, about 20 minutes. Add some water if the prunes are not tender and the liquid has reduced too quickly. Let stand until cool.

Just before making the ice cream, drain the prunes and reserve the liquid (add a little extra alcohol if there is less than ¼ cup). Cut the prunes into quarters. Stir the reserved alcohol into the cold ice cream base in step 4. Add the prunes during the last minute of freezing.

*I*n the United States, vanilla ice cream is more popular than chocolate ice cream. It is, of course, satisfying and delicious on its own, but it also makes the perfect accompaniment to so many of the desserts in this book, especially tarts, cakes, and soufflés. I include my recipe here because all too few purchased ice creams really deliver the authentic, familiar-but-exotic flavor of vanilla. I strongly recommend that you use vanilla beans, rather than extract, to make vanilla ice cream. The beans are what make a great vanilla ice cream. I use one to two beans per quart of ice cream; more than that is too much.

MAKES ABOUT 1 QUART

Special Equipment:
Instant-Read Thermometer;
Ice Cream Machine

Ice Creams,
Sorbets,
and
Granités

Chocolate Ice Cream

I add a little honey to my chocolate ice cream; it gives it a mellow-sweet flavor note behind the chocolate. I also add an extra egg yolk, because I like my ice cream rich. The customary ratio is eight to ten yolks per quart of milk or half-and-half; you can go with four yolks here if you don't want too much richness. The most important element, though, is the chocolate. Use a good-quality bittersweet chocolate (one with 60 to 65 percent cocoa solids).

MAKES ABOUT 1 QUART

Special Equipment:
Instant-Read Thermometer;
Ice Cream Machine

1 ounce (28 grams) bittersweet chocolate, chopped

⅔ cup (63 grams) unsweetened alkalized cocoa powder

2 cups (484 grams) whole milk

5 large egg yolks

¼ cup (50 grams) sugar

3½ tablespoons (73 grams) honey

1. Place the chopped chocolate in a medium bowl and set aside.

2. Place the cocoa powder in a medium saucepan and gradually whisk in the milk until smooth. Place the pan over medium heat and bring the mixture to a boil. Remove the pan from the heat and set aside.

3. Half-fill a large bowl with cold water. Add two large handfuls of ice cubes. Set this ice bath aside.

4. Whisk together the egg yolks and sugar in a medium bowl until thickened and pale, about 3 minutes. Continuing to whisk, drizzle in half of the hot milk mixture. Return this mixture to the saucepan and whisk to combine. Put the saucepan over medium heat and cook, stirring constantly with a wooden spoon, until the mixture thickens slightly and reaches 175°F on an instant-read thermometer (a path will remain when you draw your finger across the sauce-coated spoon). This should take about 4 minutes; do not allow the mixture to boil. Pour the hot mixture over the chopped chocolate. Whisk until the chocolate is completely melted and the mixture is smooth. Whisk in the honey.

5. Strain the custard mixture through a fine-mesh sieve into a medium bowl. Place the bowl in the larger bowl of ice water and stir the mixture occasionally until it is cold. (At this point, the custard can be stored, covered, in the refrigerator for up to 1 day before freezing.)

6. Pour the chilled custard into an ice cream maker and freeze according to the manufacturer's instructions. The ice cream can be served immediately or packed into an airtight container and stored in the freezer for up to 1 week.

Caramel Ice Cream

6 large egg yolks

¾ cup (150 grams) sugar

2 cups (484 grams) half-and-half

1 vanilla bean, split

Pinch of salt

1. In the bowl of an electric mixer fitted with the whisk attachment, beat the egg yolks and ¼ cup (50 grams) of the sugar on high speed for 3 minutes, or until pale yellow; set aside.

2. Place the half-and-half in a small saucepan, scrape the seeds from the vanilla bean into the pan, and add the bean. Heat over low heat while you prepare the caramel.

3. Combine the remaining ½ cup (100 grams) sugar, 2 tablespoons (29 grams) water, and the salt in a medium saucepan. Cook over medium-high heat, stirring constantly, until the sugar dissolves. Stop stirring, increase the heat to high, and boil until the syrup turns a dark amber caramel. Remove the pan from the heat and, standing away from the pan, carefully add the warm half-and-half; the mixture will bubble up and may spatter.

4. With the mixer on low speed, carefully pour half of the hot caramel into the yolk mixture and mix just until combined. Return the yolk mixture to the saucepan containing the remaining caramel and cook over medium heat, stirring constantly with a wooden spoon until the mixture thickens slightly and reaches 175°F on an instant-read thermometer (a path will remain when you draw your finger across the sauce-coated spoon). This should take about 4 minutes; do not allow the mixture to boil. Remove the pan from the heat and immediately strain the custard through a fine-mesh sieve into a medium bowl.

5. Half-fill a large bowl with cold water and add two large handfuls of ice. Set the bowl of custard in the bowl of ice water and stir occasionally until cold. (At this point, the custard can be stored, covered, in the refrigerator for up to 1 day before freezing.)

6. Pour the chilled mixture into an ice cream maker and freeze according to the manufacturer's instructions. The ice cream can be served immediately or packed into an airtight container and stored in the freezer for up to 1 week.

*C*aramel's distinct nutty-sweet flavor is the perfect accompaniment to so many desserts. Most people tend to undercook caramel. But a good caramel has just a touch of bitterness. You have to cook it until it turns dark amber; only then is the full flavor developed. I also suggest that you make some additional caramel, pour it out onto a baking sheet, and when it is cooled, chop it into little pieces. Then add that to the ice cream when it first comes out of the machine and is still soft. I served it that way at Le Bernardin and the customers loved it. This ice cream goes well with apricot, pear, chocolate desserts—many things.

MAKES ABOUT 1 QUART

Special Equipment:
Instant-Read Thermometer;
Ice Cream Machine

Ice Creams,
Sorbets,
and
Granités

Praline Ice Cream

This is essentially vanilla ice cream to which I add praline paste; it has less sugar than the recipe on page 177, though, to compensate for the sweetness of the praline. Kids love the flavor of praline, and adults who are not familiar with it are always pleasantly surprised. This ice cream goes well with chocolate cakes and desserts and with acidic fruits like apricots, but not peaches—the flavor of peach is too delicate to overbalance with a sweet like this.

MAKES ABOUT 1 QUART

Special Equipment:
Instant-Read Thermometer;
Ice Cream Machine

2 cups (484 grams) half-and-half

6 large egg yolks

¼ cup (50 grams) sugar

¼ cup (75 grams) Praline Paste (page 36, or see Sources, page 225)

1. Half-fill a large bowl with cold water and add two large handfuls of ice cubes. Set this ice bath aside.

2. Bring the half-and-half to a boil in a medium saucepan over medium-high heat. Remove the pan from the heat.

3. Whisk together the egg yolks and sugar in a medium bowl until thickened and pale, about 3 minutes. Whisk in half of the hot half-and-half. Pour this mixture back into the saucepan and cook over medium heat, stirring constantly with a wooden spoon, until the mixture thickens slightly and reaches 175°F on an instant-read thermometer (a path will remain when you draw your finger across the sauce-coated spoon). This should take about 4 minutes; do not allow the mixture to boil.

4. Strain the custard through a fine-mesh sieve into a medium bowl. Whisk in the praline paste. Place the bowl in the larger bowl of ice water and stir occasionally until cold. (At this point, the custard can be kept in a covered container in the refrigerator for up to 1 day before freezing.)

5. Freeze the ice cream in an ice cream maker according to the manufacturer's instructions. The ice cream can be served immediately, or packed into an airtight container and stored in the freezer for up to 1 week.

Pistachio Ice Cream

2 cups (484 grams) half-and-half

½ vanilla bean, split

6 large egg yolks

Generous ½ cup (100 grams) sugar

½ cup (150 grams) Pistachio Paste (page 37, or see Sources, page 225)

1. Half-fill a large bowl with cold water and add two large handfuls of ice cubes. Set this ice bath aside.

2. Place the half-and-half in a medium saucepan, scrape the seeds from the vanilla bean into the pan, and add the bean. Bring to a boil over medium-high heat. Remove the pan from the heat.

3. Whisk together the egg yolks and sugar in a medium bowl until thickened and pale yellow, about 3 minutes. Whisk half of the hot half-and-half mixture into the yolks. Pour this mixture back into the saucepan and whisk to combine. Place the pan over medium heat and cook, stirring constantly with a wooden spoon, until the mixture thickens slightly and reaches 175°F on an instant-read thermometer (a path will remain in the sauce when you draw your finger across the sauce-coated spoon). This should take about 4 minutes; do not allow the mixture to boil. Strain the custard through a fine-mesh sieve into a medium bowl and whisk in the pistachio paste.

4. Place the bowl in the large bowl of ice water and stir occasionally until it is cold. (At this point, the custard can be kept in a covered container in the refrigerator for up to 1 day before freezing.)

5. Freeze the ice cream in an ice cream maker according to the manufacturer's instructions. The ice cream can be served immediately, or packed into an airtight container and stored in the freezer for up to 1 week.

*W*ith its subtle but unmistakable flavor of pistachio, this ice cream is good served with berries, especially raspberries, and a great accompaniment to most of the chocolate cakes in this book. But if you want something really special, chop up some additional pistachios, put them in a bowl, and roll scoops of the ice cream in them until coated. All that crunch with the silky ice cream is what dessert is all about.

MAKES ABOUT 1 QUART

Special Equipment:
Instant-Read Thermometer;
Ice Cream Machine

*Ice Creams,
Sorbets,
and
Granités*

181

Strawberry Sorbet

This is so simple—just strawberries and sugar syrup, for a sorbet that is the essence of the fruit. I always add just a little bit of lemon juice, because it actually enhances the flavor of strawberry. If you want to be creative, you could add lemongrass to your stock, just a touch. (Add minced lemongrass to the syrup and strain before using.) Serve this with fresh berries. You can even add it to a blender with vanilla ice cream for a shake.

MAKES ABOUT 1 QUART

Special Equipment:
Ice Cream Machine

⅔ cup (134 grams) sugar

1 pint (226 grams) strawberries, washed, hulled, and cut into quarters

Juice of ½ lemon

1. Combine the sugar and ½ cup (118 grams) water in a medium saucepan. Bring to a boil over medium-high heat, stirring to dissolve the sugar. Remove the pan from the heat and pour the syrup into a medium bowl. Refrigerate until cool, about 1 hour.

2. Place the strawberries in the bowl of a food processor and process until smooth. Add the lemon juice and process until combined. Stir the strawberry purée into the cool sugar syrup and refrigerate until well chilled, about 2 hours and up to 24 hours.

3. Freeze the sorbet in an ice cream maker according to the manufacturer's instructions. Serve immediately, or pack into an airtight container and store in the freezer for up to 1 week.

Mango Sorbet

2 mangoes, peeled, pitted, and cut into chunks

½ cup (100 grams) sugar

Juice of 2 limes

1. Place the mango chunks in the bowl of a food processor and process to a smooth purée. Refrigerate the purée until ready to use.

2. Combine the sugar and ¾ cup (177 grams) water in a medium saucepan. Bring to a boil over medium-high heat, stirring to dissolve the sugar. Remove the pan from the heat and pour the syrup into a medium bowl. Refrigerate until cool, about 1 hour.

3. Stir the mango purée and lime juice into the cold syrup. Refrigerate the sorbet mixture until well chilled, about 2 hours. (At this point, the mixture can be stored in an airtight container in the refrigerator for up to 24 hours.)

4. Freeze the sorbet in an ice cream machine according to the manufacturer's instructions. Serve immediately, or pack into an airtight container and store in the freezer for up to 1 week.

*S*orbet is the perfect way to deliver the tantalizing flavor of mango, and its bright orange color makes it the ideal centerpiece of any sorbet assortment. Serve in Mango Soup with Gingered Raspberries (page 51) or with pound cake.

MAKES ABOUT 1 QUART

Special Equipment:
Ice Cream Machine

*Ice Creams,
Sorbets,
and
Granités*

Citrus Sorbet

My recipe for Winter Fruit Soup is on page 52; this is another way to play with the same easy-to-find winter fruits—grapefruit, orange, lime, and banana. The banana is an important element, because when you blend so much citrus together for the sorbet, you have to add water to cut the acidity. Without the banana, the texture is too much like that of an ice. And the banana isn't acidic, so it balances the flavor as well as the texture. This sorbet goes well with the Winter Fruit Soup, of course, or you can serve it with pound cake. Grown-ups might also like it with a splash of vodka over it.

MAKES ABOUT 1½ PINTS

Special Equipment:
Ice Cream Machine

⅔ cup (134 grams) sugar

½ banana, peeled

1 cup (242 grams) fresh orange juice

1 cup (242 grams) fresh grapefruit juice

½ cup (125 grams) fresh lime juice

2 tablespoons (30 grams) grenadine

1. Combine the sugar and ½ cup (118 grams) water in a medium saucepan. Bring to a boil over medium heat, stirring to dissolve the sugar. Remove the pan from the heat and pour the syrup into a medium bowl. Refrigerate until chilled, about 2 hours.

2. Place the banana in a food processor and process until smooth. Add the citrus juices and grenadine and process until combined. Stir into the chilled sugar syrup.

3. Freeze the sorbet in an ice cream maker according to the manufacturer's instructions. Serve immediately, or pack into an airtight container and store in the freezer for up to 1 week.

Ice Creams,
Sorbets,
and
Granités

Chocolate Sorbet

4 ounces (113 grams) bittersweet chocolate, chopped

¾ cup (150 grams) sugar

¾ cup (71 grams) unsweetened alkalized cocoa powder, sifted

3 tablespoons (43 grams) heavy cream

1 teaspoon (4 grams) pure vanilla extract

1. Place the chocolate in a medium bowl; set aside.

2. Half-fill a large bowl with cold water. Add two large handfuls of ice cubes and set this ice bath aside.

3. Combine the sugar and 2⅓ cups (550 grams) water in a medium saucepan. Cook, stirring constantly, until the mixture comes to a boil. Whisk in the cocoa powder and boil for another minute. Pour the hot syrup over the chocolate and whisk until the chocolate is completely melted and the mixture is smooth. Strain through a fine-mesh sieve into a medium bowl. Refrigerate until chilled, about 2 hours.

4. Whisk the heavy cream and vanilla into the chocolate mixture. Pour into an ice cream maker and freeze according to the manufacturer's instructions. Serve immediately or pack into an airtight container and store in the freezer for up to 1 week.

*W*hen you want something chocolate, but you want something light, this is the answer. A touch of cream at the end mellows the flavor and adds a touch of richness. You can substitute water, but I recommend the cream. Serve with chocolate cakes or with an assortment of other sorbets.

MAKES ABOUT 1 QUART

Special Equipment:
Ice Cream Machine

Ice Creams,
Sorbets,
and
Granités

185

Peach-Verbena Granité

I don't usually like to combine peach with anything; its flavor is nature's perfection. But I was fooling around with verbena one day—I was challenged by its volatile, lemony flavor—and this combination set off such sparks in my mouth, I couldn't resist. Follow the recipe exactly; just a hint of verbena is all that is needed to produce those sparks.

MAKES 12 SERVINGS

8 (about 4 pounds) (1.8 kilos) ripe peaches plus 1 peach cut into 12 slices, for garnish

1 cup (200 grams) sugar

30 dried verbena leaves (see page 11)

Juice of 1½ to 2 lemons, or to taste

12 mint sprigs

1. Half-fill a large bowl with ice water. Add two large handfuls of ice cubes and set aside.

2. *Blanch the peaches:* Using a paring knife, cut a small X in the skin at the bottom and top of each peach. Combine 4 cups (944 grams) water, the sugar, and the verbena leaves in a large saucepan and bring to a boil. Add the peaches and blanch for 2 minutes. Transfer the peaches with a slotted spoon to the ice water to cool. Set the blanching liquid aside to steep for 2 hours.

3. Remove the peaches from the ice water and allow them to drain on paper towels. Peel the peaches, using the tip of a paring knife. Cut the peaches in half, remove the pits, and cut into cubes.

4. Put the peach cubes in a blender or food processor. Add the blanching liquid, pouring it through a sieve. Process the mixture until smooth. Add lemon juice to your taste. Pour the mixture into a stainless steel (nonreactive) baking pan (an 8- or 9-inch square pan is fine), cover, and freeze until firm, at least 8 hours, or overnight. (You can make the granité ahead and keep it covered in the freezer for up to 3 days.)

5. Using the tip of a spoon or the tines of a fork, scrape the granité into chilled dessert glasses. Serve immediately, garnished with the peach slices and mint sprigs.

Melon-Lime Granité

⅔ cup (134 grams) sugar

¼ cup (8 grams) Kaffir lime leaves (see Note)

1 stalk lemongrass, coarsely chopped (see Note); if no lemongrass, use 1 teaspoon of finely grated lime zest

1 large (about 3½ pounds) (1.6 kilos) very ripe honeydew melon, peeled, seeded, and cut into 1-inch chunks, plus 12 small slices for garnish

Juice of 2 limes

*T*his is a perfect flavor combination for a granité, refreshing and a great wake-up call for your senses on a hot day. The mellow flavor of melon is enlivened by the tangy spike of lime, through lime juice and Kaffir lime leaves.

MAKES 12 SERVINGS

1. Combine the sugar, ⅔ cup (157 grams) water, the lime leaves, and lemongrass in a small saucepan. Bring to a boil over medium-high heat, stirring until the sugar dissolves. Remove from the heat and let the syrup steep for 1 hour.

2. Process the melon chunks in a blender or food processor until smooth. Strain the sugar syrup into the purée and add the lime juice. Process until well blended. Pour the mixture into a shallow metal baking pan (an 8- or 9-inch pan will do fine), cover, and freeze until firm, at least 8 hours, and up to 3 days in advance.

3. Use a fork or the tip of a spoon to scrape the granité into chilled martini glasses. Garnish each with a melon slice and serve immediately, as this melts very quickly.

NOTE: Kaffir lime leaves and lemongrass are available at Thai markets.

Ice Creams,
Sorbets,
and
Granités

Pink Champagne and Raspberry Granité

In France, we love our champagne. But to be honest, the inspiration for this granité was more the color of champagne and raspberries—it looks so pretty. Happily, it tastes fantastic too. This can be served with fresh berries, and it makes an ideal pre-dessert course. People tend to think pink champagne means one of those too-sweet sparkling wines, but a good rosé champagne can be fabulous.

MAKES 6 TO 8 SERVINGS

2½ pints (565 grams) raspberries
1⅓ cups (266 grams) sugar
One 750-ml bottle rosé champagne
Juice of 1 lemon

1. Combine 2 pints (452 grams) of the raspberries, the sugar, and ¼ cup (59 grams) water in a medium saucepan. Bring to a boil over medium-high heat, stirring to dissolve the sugar. Transfer the mixture to a blender or food processor and process until smooth.

2. Strain the purée through a fine-mesh sieve into a large bowl. Stir in the champagne and lemon juice. Scrape the mixture into a shallow metal baking pan (an 8- or 9-inch pan is fine), cover, and freeze until firm, at least 8 hours, or overnight. (You can make the granité ahead and keep it covered in the freezer for up to 3 days.)

3. Using the tip of a spoon or the tines of a fork, scrape the granité into chilled dessert glasses and serve immediately, garnished with the remaining ½ pint (113 grams) raspberries.

Pink Champagne and Raspberry Granité

Holiday Cakes, Cookies, and Bites

Because it is woven into a particular holiday memory, my favorite holiday cake is the Chestnut Bûche de Noël, which is a variation of the more traditional Chocolate Bûche. *Bûche de Noël* translates as "Yule log," and the cakes are formed to resemble logs. When I was a kid, my father's twenty-foot prep table would be covered end-to-end with these logs at holiday time. It was as if our humble bakeshop provided all of Nice with Bûches de Noël. As a youngster, I was not much help in the family business, but in December I would often march into the shop, tug on my father's jacket, and say, "Can I help you?" He knew what I meant. He would hoist me onto a stepstool and let me apply the little plastic toy that came with each log. (In our New York shop today, we can't put a plastic toy on a log because, by law, all decorations have to be edible.)

With these recipes, I have tried to offer a variety of desserts, some perhaps new to you, appropriate for both festive occasions of all kinds, such as birthdays and many of the major holidays, including Thanksgiving. There's always pumpkin pie, of course, but the Deep Chocolate Holiday Cake might become a welcome companion to that American classic. You will find recipes for some holidays you might never have thought to bake for, like Valentine's Day. And two of these recipes are traditionally served in France at Carnival time, but you can serve them any time you like.

Bunny Cake

Coconut Syrup

½ cup (100 grams) sugar

3 tablespoons (50 grams) coconut liqueur, such as Malibu

Assembly

Two 9-inch round Génoises (page 27)

1 recipe Vanilla Buttercream (page 30)

1½ cups (100 grams) sweetened shredded coconut

A few drops of red food coloring

2 M & M's

Assorted fruit jelly candies

3 vanilla beans, split

1. *Make the coconut syrup:* Combine the sugar and ½ cup (100 grams) water in a small saucepan. Bring to a boil over medium-high heat, stirring to dissolve the sugar. Remove the pan from the heat and stir in the coconut liqueur.

2. *Assemble the cake:* Using a long serrated knife, cut each cake horizontally into three even layers. Place the two top layers cut side up on two 8¾-inch cardboard cake rounds. Using a pastry brush, generously moisten the cakes with the coconut syrup. Fill a pastry bag fitted with a ½-inch plain tip with the buttercream. Pipe a wide spiral of buttercream on top of the cake layers and smooth it into a thin layer with a small, offset metal spatula. Place the two middle layers on top of the buttercream. Moisten the layers with coconut syrup and pipe and spread another layer of buttercream on top. Place the bottom layers of the cakes on a work surface, cut side up, and brush them generously with the coconut syrup. Invert the layers onto the cakes, so that the cut sides are against the buttercream. Press down firmly on the tops. Using an offset spatula, spread buttercream evenly over the top and sides of the cakes. Set the remaining buttercream aside. Chill the cakes for 30 minutes.

3. Using a sharp knife, cut away two ear-shaped semicircles from two opposite sides of one of the cakes, leaving a bow-tie shaped cake in the center, and set aside. Place the other cake—the head—on a platter. Arrange the two ear shapes at the top of the head and the bow tie shape below the head. Spread the sides of the ears and bow tie with the remaining buttercream.

continued

*T*his is my wife's recipe. I have never seen anything like it in Europe. Since she was a girl, Alex has made this in the shape of either a mouse (she is a big fan of Mickey Mouse) or a bunny. When I first went up to Nyack, New York, to meet her parents, she made this for me, and I found it so funny, I had to go outside to recover. You make two round cakes. One is left whole while the other is cut to form the ears and the bow tie, which you arrange around the round cake, and decorate accordingly. It sounds silly, but it's fun and easy to do. Now, Alex's recipe needed . . . help. I had to change it to make it edible, but the idea is still hers. It is now génoise brushed with coconut liqueur and iced with vanilla buttercream. It is wonderful served with Vanilla Ice Cream (page 177). Obviously, it's perfect for Easter.

MAKES 16 TO 20 SERVINGS

Special Equipment:
Two 9-Inch Cardboard Cake Rounds Trimmed to 8¾ Inches; Pastry Bag Fitted with a ½-Inch Plain Tip (Such as Ateco #6)

Holiday Cakes, Cookies, and Bites

4. Put ⅓ cup (22 grams) of the coconut into a small resealable plastic bag. In a small cup, dilute one or two drops of the red food coloring with ½ teaspoon (2 grams) water. Pour the diluted coloring into the plastic bag, seal, and shake the bag until the coconut is tinted an even pink. Pat the pink coconut down in the center of each ear. Cover the rest of the ears, the bunny head, and the bow tie with the untinted coconut.

5. Create the bunny face by using the M & M's for eyes, fruit jelly candies for the nose and mouth, and the vanilla bean halves for whiskers.

NOTE: The génoise cake and the buttercream can be made and stored, well wrapped in the refrigerator, for up to three days in advance. The bunny cake can be assembled up to one day in advance and stored in the refrigerator. Bring to room temperature before serving.

Holiday Cakes,
Cookies,
and Bites

Bunny Cake 193

Fraisier

Fraisier is a traditional cake for Valentine's Day in France. It is very simple: A génoise brushed with raspberry syrup is filled with mousseline, an enriched pastry cream, and then topped with buttercream. French pastry shops often make the cake in a heart-shaped mold; for another Valentine's touch, you can tint the buttercream pink. It is decorated with strawberries; you could dip the whole strawberries for the garnish in chocolate, if you like. This version is also a wonderful birthday cake for a young girl. It can be made a day ahead.

MAKE 8 TO 10 SERVINGS

Special Equipment:
9-Inch Springform Pan;
9-Inch Cardboard Cake Round;
Pastry Bag Fitted with a ½-Inch
Plain Tip (Such as Ateco #6)

Berry Syrup

¼ cup (50 grams) sugar

½ cup (56 grams) mixed berries, such as strawberries, raspberries, and blackberries

Crème Mousseline

9 tablespoons (128 grams) unsalted butter, softened

1 cup (250 grams) Pastry Cream (page 28)

Assembly

One 9-inch round Génoise (page 27)

37 large strawberries, washed and hulled, 12 cut lengthwise in half, 25 left whole

1 cup (200 grams) Vanilla Buttercream (page 30)

1. *Make the berry syrup:* Combine the sugar and ¼ cup (59 grams) water in a small saucepan. Bring to a boil over medium-high heat, stirring to dissolve the sugar. Let the syrup cool to room temperature.

2. Place the berries and cooled sugar syrup in a blender or food processor and process until smooth. Pass the berry purée through a fine-mesh sieve into a medium bowl and set aside.

3. *Make the crème mousseline:* In the bowl of an electric mixer, using the paddle attachment, beat the butter at medium-high speed for 2 minutes, until light and creamy. Add the pastry cream and beat at medium speed until combined, scraping down the side of the bowl with a rubber spatula once or twice. Set aside at room temperature.

4. *Assemble the cake:* Replace the metal bottom of the springform pan with a 9-inch cardboard round and attach the side. Line the side of the pan with a strip of parchment paper.

5. Using a long serrated knife, cut the génoise cake horizontally in half. Place the top layer, cut side up, in the pan. Brush the cake generously with the berry syrup. Fill a pastry bag fitted with a ½-inch plain tip with the crème mousseline and pipe a thick layer onto the cake. Spread it into a smooth layer with a small offset spatula.

6. Stand the strawberry halves, points up and cut sides out, around the side of the pan. Arrange the whole strawberries, points up, in the center of the cake, pushing them lightly into the mousseline. Pipe a layer of mousseline over the strawberries, filling in any gaps between them.

7. Place the other génoise layer cut side up on a work surface and brush generously with the berry syrup. Invert the layer onto the mousse-line layer and press down firmly on it. Using an offset metal spatula, smooth the buttercream evenly over the top of the cake. Refrigerate the cake for at least 45 minutes and up to 8 hours in advance.

8. *Serve the cake:* Remove the side of the springform pan and peel off the strip of parchment paper. Serve the cake chilled, cutting it with a hot knife to make clean slices (dip the knife in hot water and wipe dry between cuts).

David and I work on a new dish.

*Holiday Cakes,
Cookies,
and Bites*

Chocolate Yule Log

The Bûche de Noël is always a show-stopper, as much holiday decor as it is dessert. Here are three variations. This chocolate one is for the kids; there is no alcohol, of course, but plenty of chocolate: chocolate pastry cream, chocolate syrup in the cake, chocolate glaze to simulate the bark. Some cakes are better when made a day ahead to give the flavors a chance to develop. That is true of this cake. Both this chocolate log and the two variations can be made the day before they are to be served, and refrigerated. All three can be served with Vanilla Ice Cream (page 177), or perhaps some whipped cream, but the chocolate and chestnut cakes are also fine all by themselves.

MAKES 8 TO 10 SERVINGS

Génoise

5 large eggs

1¼ cups (150 grams) sugar

1 cup (130 grams) cake flour, sifted

2 tablespoons (28 grams) unsalted butter, melted

Chocolate Pastry Cream

½ cup (100 grams) sugar

¼ cup (24 grams) unsweetened alkalized cocoa powder, sifted

1 cup (242 grams) whole milk

½ vanilla bean, split

3 large egg yolks

2 tablespoons (15 grams) cornstarch, sifted

Cocoa Syrup

½ cup (100 grams) sugar

¼ cup (25 grams) unsweetened cocoa powder, sifted

Chocolate Glaze

11 ounces (312 grams) bittersweet chocolate, finely chopped

1¼ cups (290 grams) heavy cream

Garnish

White chocolate stars (see page 20)

Meringue Mushrooms (page 35)

Chocolate fans (see page 20)

Chocolate truffles, optional

1. *Make the génoise:* Preheat the oven to 400°F. Line a 10 × 15-inch jelly-roll pan with parchment paper.

2. Fill a medium saucepan one-third full with water and bring to a simmer. In the bowl of an electric mixer, whisk together the eggs and sugar by hand. Place the bowl over the pan of simmering water and whisk constantly until the mixture is warm to the touch. Transfer the bowl to the mixer stand. Using the whisk attachment, beat at medium-high speed until the mixture has doubled in volume and is cool, about 7 minutes. Using a rubber spatula, gently fold in the cake flour.

3. Place the melted butter in a small bowl. Stir a large scoop of the

continued

Chocolate Yule Log

cake batter into the butter until well combined. Gently fold this mixture into the remaining cake batter. Scrape the batter into the prepared jelly-roll pan. Smooth the top with an offset metal spatula.

4. Bake the cake for 5 to 7 minutes, until the top is light golden brown and springs back when lightly touched. Don't overbake the cake, or it will be dry. Place a wire rack over the cake, invert, and cool completely, leaving the parchment paper on the cake.

5. *Make the chocolate pastry cream:* Put ¼ cup (50 grams) of the sugar and the cocoa powder in a medium saucepan. Gradually whisk in the milk, about 2 tablespoons at a time, until well combined and smooth. Scrape the seeds from the vanilla bean into the pan, add the bean, and bring to a boil over medium-high heat. Remove the pan from the heat and set aside.

6. Whisk together the egg yolks, the remaining ¼ cup (50 grams) sugar, and the cornstarch in a medium bowl until thickened and pale. Gradually whisk in about half of the hot milk until blended. Return the mixture to the saucepan and cook over medium heat, whisking constantly, until the pastry cream boils and thickens. Continue to cook, whisking constantly, for another minute. Remove the pan from the heat and remove the vanilla bean. Scrape the pastry cream into a medium bowl, place a piece of plastic wrap directly against the surface of the cream to prevent a skin from forming, and refrigerate until chilled, about 2 hours.

7. *Make the cocoa syrup:* Combine the sugar and cocoa powder in a small saucepan. Gradually whisk in ½ cup (118 grams) water until smooth. Bring to a boil over medium-high heat. Remove the pan from the heat and cool the syrup completely.

8. Strain the syrup through a sieve into a small container and set aside.

9. *Assemble the cake:* Place the cake right side up on a work surface. Brush it generously with the cocoa syrup. Scrape about 1 cup of the chocolate pastry cream onto the cake and, using an offset metal spatula, spread it into an even layer. Starting at one of the long sides, roll the cake up tightly, peeling off the parchment paper as you roll. Rewrap the rolled cake in the parchment paper, twisting the ends tightly to secure them. Freeze the cake for 1 hour.

10. Slice an angled piece from each end of the log. Glue the two pieces together with a small amount of pastry cream to form a small stump. Attach the stump to the top of the cake with some of the pastry cream. Spread the remaining pastry cream over the entire log in a thin layer. Freeze the cake for 20 minutes.

11. *Make the chocolate glaze:* Put the chocolate in a medium bowl. Bring the heavy cream to a boil in a medium saucepan over medium-high heat. Pour the hot cream over the chocolate and gently stir until the chocolate is completely melted and the mixture is smooth.

12. Place the chilled log on a wire rack over a large baking sheet. Pour the warm glaze evenly over the log, coating it completely. Refrigerate the log for at least 20 minutes, or up to 8 hours in advance.

13. *Garnish the cake:* Garnish the top of the log as desired with white chocolate stars, meringue mushrooms, chocolate fans, and the optional chocolate truffles. Serve chilled.

Chestnut Yule Log

Chestnut Yule Log

Génoise

5 large eggs

1¼ cups (250 grams) sugar

1 cup (130 grams) cake flour, sifted

2 tablespoons (28 grams) unsalted butter, melted

Chestnut Pastry Cream

⅔ cup (160 grams) whole milk

½ vanilla bean, split

2 large egg yolks

¼ cup plus 2 tablespoons (75 grams) sugar

2 tablespoons (15 grams) cornstarch

½ cup (136 grams) sweetened chestnut purée (see Sources, page 225)

1 tablespoon (14 grams) dark rum, such as Myers's, or whiskey

Ginger Syrup

1¼ cups (250 grams) sugar

2 tablespoons (30 grams) peeled and chopped ginger

Assembly

1 cup (232 grams) heavy cream

10 candied chestnuts, coarsely chopped (see Sources, page 225)

Garnish

½ cup (47 grams) unsweetened cocoa powder

White chocolate leaves (see page 20)

Meringue Mushrooms (page 35)

*C*hestnuts are an integral part of the December holidays, especially in France but in America as well. Before rolling the sponge cake up with the chestnut cream filling, I brush it with ginger syrup, adding a slight tingle that goes so well with chestnut. The pieces of whole candied chestnut in the chestnut cream make for a wonderful surprise when you bite into the cake.

MAKES 8 TO 10 SERVINGS

---

1. *Make the génoise:* Preheat the oven to 400°F. Line a 10 × 15-inch jelly-roll pan with parchment paper.

2. Fill a medium saucepan one-third full with water and bring to a simmer. In the bowl of an electric mixer, whisk together the eggs and sugar by hand. Place the bowl over the pan of simmering water and whisk constantly until the mixture is warm to the touch. Transfer the bowl to the mixer stand. Using the whisk attachment, beat at medium-high speed until the egg mixture has doubled in volume and is cool, about 7 minutes. Using a rubber spatula, gently fold in the cake flour.

continued

*Holiday Cakes,
Cookies,
and Bites*

3. Place the melted butter in a small bowl. Stir a large scoop of the cake batter into the butter until well combined. Gently fold this mixture into the remaining cake batter. Scrape the batter into the prepared jelly-roll pan. Smooth the top with an offset metal spatula.

4. Bake the cake for 5 to 7 minutes, until the top is light golden brown and springs back when lightly touched. Don't overbake the cake, or it will be dry. Immediately invert the cake onto a wire rack and cool completely, leaving the parchment paper on the cake.

5. *Make the chestnut pastry cream:* Put the milk in a medium saucepan. Scrape the seeds from the vanilla bean into the pan, and add the bean. Bring to a boil over medium-high heat. Remove the pan from the heat and set aside.

6. Whisk together the egg yolks, sugar, and cornstarch in a medium bowl until pale yellow. Gradually whisk in about half of the hot milk until blended. Return the mixture to the saucepan and cook over medium heat, whisking constantly, until the pastry cream boils and thickens. Continue to cook, whisking constantly, for another minute. Remove the pan from the heat and whisk in the chestnut purée and rum. Remove the vanilla bean. Scrape the pastry cream into a bowl, place a piece of plastic wrap directly against the surface to prevent a skin from forming, and refrigerate until chilled, about 2 hours.

7. *Make the ginger syrup:* Combine the sugar, 1 cup (236 grams) water, and the ginger in a small saucepan and bring to a boil. Remove the pan from the heat and cool the syrup completely. Strain the syrup through a sieve into a small container and set aside.

8. *Assemble the cake:* In the bowl of an electric mixer, using the whisk attachment, beat the heavy cream at high speed to soft peaks. Fold about one third of the whipped cream into the pastry cream to lighten it. Gently fold in the remaining whipped cream. Cover and refrigerate until ready to assemble the cake, up to 1 day in advance.

9. Place the cake right side up on a work surface. Brush it generously with the ginger syrup. Scrape about 1 cup of the pastry cream onto the cake and, using an offset metal spatula, spread it into an even layer. Arrange the candied chestnut pieces down one long side of the cake, about 2 inches from the edge. Starting at this side, roll the cake up tightly, peeling off the parchment paper as you roll. Rewrap the rolled cake in the parchment paper, twisting the ends tightly to secure them. Freeze the cake for 1 hour.

10. Slice an angled piece from each end of the log. Glue the two pieces together with a small amount of the chestnut cream to form a small stump. Attach the stump to the top of the cake with some of the chestnut cream. Spread the remaining chestnut cream over the entire log, smoothing it into an even layer. Run a pastry comb or fork lengthwise down the log and stump several times so the frosting resembles tree bark. Dip your finger into the cocoa and touch it to the center of one of the ends of the log. Repeat with the other end. Dip a glass in the cocoa and stamp a cocoa circle around each fingerprint, to look like the cross-section of a log. Garnish the top of the log with white chocolate leaves and meringue mushrooms. Serve chilled.

Raspberry Yule Log

This cake, which is like a deluxe jelly roll, is the lightest of the three bûches, but it is still fairly rich. The apples cooked with the raspberries for the filling add pectin, which helps firm the mixture.

MAKES 8 TO 10 SERVINGS

Sponge Cake

5 large eggs

1¼ cups (250 grams) sugar

1 cup (130 grams) cake flour, sifted

2 tablespoons (28 grams) unsalted butter, melted

Raspberry Filling

3 medium (510 grams) Golden Delicious apples, peeled, cored, and cut into small dice

½ cup (100 grams) sugar

1 pint (226 grams) raspberries

Raspberry Syrup

½ cup (120 grams) Simple Syrup (page 38)

2 tablespoons (30 grams) eau-de-framboise or other raspberry liqueur

Whipped Cream Frosting

1 cup (232 grams) heavy cream

½ cup (57 grams) confectioners' sugar

1. *Make the sponge cake:* Preheat the oven to 400°F. Line a 10 × 15-inch jelly-roll pan with parchment paper.

2. Fill a medium saucepan one-third full with water and bring to a simmer. In the bowl of an electric mixer, whisk together the eggs and sugar by hand. Place the bowl over the pan of simmering water and whisk constantly until the mixture is warm to the touch. Transfer the bowl to the mixer stand. Using the whisk attachment, beat at medium-high speed until the egg mixture has doubled in volume and is cool, about 7 minutes. Using a rubber spatula, gently fold in the cake flour.

3. Place the melted butter in a small bowl. Stir a large scoop of the cake batter into the butter until well combined. Gently fold this mixture into the remaining cake batter. Scrape the batter into the prepared jelly-roll pan. Smooth the top with an offset metal spatula.

4. Bake the cake for 5 to 7 minutes, until the top is light golden brown and springs back when lightly touched. Don't overbake the cake, or it will be dry. Immediately invert the cake onto a wire rack and cool completely, leaving the parchment paper on the cake.

5. *Make the raspberry filling:* Combine the diced apples and sugar in a medium saucepan. Cook over low heat, covered, until the apples are translucent, about 5 minutes. Stir in the raspberries. Cook, stirring occasionally, for 5 minutes, until the raspberries are softened. Transfer the mixture to a blender and process until smooth.

6. Return the mixture to the saucepan. Bring to a boil over medium-high heat. Remove from the heat and set aside to cool.

7. *Make the raspberry syrup:* Stir together the simple syrup and eau-de-framboise in a small bowl; set aside.

8. *Make the whipped cream frosting:* In the bowl of an electric mixer, using the whisk attachment, beat the cream with the confectioners' sugar at high speed to stiff peaks. Refrigerate until ready to frost the cake.

9. *Assemble the cake:* Place the cake right side up on a work surface. Brush it generously with the raspberry syrup. Spread the raspberry filling over the cake, covering it completely. Starting at one of the long sides, roll the cake up tightly, peeling off the parchment paper as you roll. Rewrap the rolled cake in the paper, twisting the ends tightly to secure them. Freeze the cake for 1 hour.

10. Slice an angled piece from each end of the log. Glue the two pieces together with a small amount of the whipped cream to form a small stump. Attach the stump to the top of the cake with some of the whipped cream. Spread a thin layer of the whipped cream over the entire log. Return the log to the freezer for 20 minutes. Refrigerate the remaining whipped cream.

11. Spread the remaining whipped cream over the log. Run a pastry comb or fork lengthwise down the log and stump several times so the cream resembles tree bark. Serve the cake chilled.

Opera Cake

*T*his classic French cake was developed by the famous pâtissier Gaston Lenôtre, but the recipe has been abused over the years. In a true Opera Cake, you should never see the layers of the yellow sponge. The coffee syrup should disguise it. So don't be afraid to drench the cake with plenty of the syrup. It boosts the flavor and adds moisture. This cake is for New Year's Eve; we decorate it with a calendar made from piped white and dark chocolates. It also works for Father's Day, when the decoration is a shirt and tie; Mother's Day, with a blouse with a bow; even for a new baby: a rattle and bow.

MAKES 24 SERVINGS

Special Equipment:
Three 10 × 15-Inch
Jelly-Roll Pans; 9 × 14-Inch
Cardboard Cake Board

Holiday Cakes,
Cookies,
and Bites

Cake

8 large eggs, separated, at room temperature

4 large egg yolks, at room temperature

2⅓ cups (466 grams) sugar

Pinch of salt

Scant 2 cups (280 grams) all-purpose flour, sifted

⅔ cup (129 grams) Clarified Butter, melted (page 38)

Coffee Syrup

1 tablespoon (2 grams) instant espresso powder or instant coffee granules

1 cup (200 grams) sugar

Ganache

1 pound (454 grams) bittersweet chocolate, finely chopped

2 cups (464 grams) heavy cream

Assembly

3 cups (600 grams) Mocha Buttercream (page 30)

1. *Make the cake:* Preheat the oven to 425°F. Arrange two baking racks near the center of the oven. Lightly butter the bottoms and sides of three 10 × 15-inch jelly-roll pans and line the bottoms of the pans with parchment paper. Dust the sides of the pans with flour and tap out the excess.

2. In an electric mixer, using the whisk attachment, beat the 12 egg yolks and sugar at medium speed until combined. Increase the speed to high and beat until thickened and pale, about 3 minutes. Transfer to a large bowl.

3. In a clean dry mixer bowl, using the clean dry whisk attachment, beat the egg whites and salt on low speed until foamy. Gradually increase the speed to high, beating just until the whites form soft peaks when the whisk is lifted. Fold the whites into the yolks in three additions, alternating them with the flour in three additions.

4. Put the clarified butter in a medium bowl. Stir a large scoop of the batter into the butter until combined. Gently fold this mixture into the remaining batter. Scrape the batter into the prepared pans, dividing it evenly, and, using a spatula, quickly spread the batter into an even layer.

5. Place one cake on the upper rack and two on the lower rack. Bake the cake layers for 10 to 12 minutes, until the edges pull away from the sides of the pan and the tops spring back when lightly touched. (The cake on the upper rack may be done before the cakes on the lower rack—watch carefully.) Invert the layers onto wire racks, peel off the parchment paper, and cool completely.

6. *Make the coffee syrup:* Dissolve the espresso powder in 2 teaspoons (10 grams) water. Combine the sugar and ¾ cup (177 grams) water in a medium saucepan. Bring to a boil over medium-high heat, stirring until the sugar is completely dissolved. Remove the pan from the heat and stir in the coffee. Let cool completely.

7. *Make the ganache:* Put the chocolate in a large bowl. Bring the cream to a boil in a medium saucepan over medium-high heat. Pour the hot cream over the chocolate and whisk until the chocolate is completely melted and the ganache is smooth. Transfer half of the ganache to a medium bowl. Place the bowl in the refrigerator and chill, stirring occasionally, until it is spreadable, about 1½ hours (this is the filling). Reserve the other half of the ganache at room temperature (this will be used to glaze the cake).

8. *Assemble the cake:* Place one of the cake layers on a 9 × 14-inch cardboard cake rectangle and set it on an inverted baking sheet. Brush the cake generously with the coffee syrup. Scrape the chilled ganache filling onto the cake and spread it into a thin even layer with an offset spatula. Place a second cake layer over the ganache layer. Brush generously with coffee syrup. Scrape half of the mocha buttercream onto the cake layer and spread it into a thin even layer with the offset spatula. Refrigerate the cake for 20 minutes.

9. Place the third cake layer over the buttercream layer, right side up. Brush generously with coffee syrup. Scrape the remaining mocha buttercream onto the top of the cake and spread it into a thin even layer. Freeze the cake for 30 minutes.

10. Fill a medium saucepan one-third full with water and bring to a simmer. Set the bowl of ganache over the water and stir just until it is warm. Remove the cake from the freezer and place it on a wire cooling rack set over a baking sheet. Pour the warm glaze over the cake, smoothing the top with an offset spatula. Let the glaze set for 10 minutes.

11. Using a long serrated knife, trim about ¼ inch off the sides of the cake so that you can see the layers. Cut the cake into 3 × 1½-inch rectangles with a hot dry knife (dip the knife in hot water and wipe clean between cuts). The cake may be made up to 1 day in advance and stored in the refrigerator. Let it come to room temperature before serving.

Holiday Cakes,
Cookies,
and Bites

Heart-Shaped Linzer Cookies

In France, as in America, Valentine's Day is an important holiday. During that passionate time of year, people come into my shop in New York, as they did my father's, and ask for something red. Heart-shaped linzer cookies are the answer. This is a sweet cookie filled with raspberry jam. Simple, traditional, and delicious.

MAKES ABOUT 20 COOKIES

Special Equipment:
2½-Inch Heart-Shaped Cookie Cutter; 1-Inch Heart-Shaped Cutter

½ pound plus 1 tablespoon (2 sticks plus 1 tablespoon) (240 grams) unsalted butter, softened

½ cup (100 grams) sugar

2 teaspoons (4 grams) ground cinnamon

1 cup (89 grams) hazelnut flour (see Sources, page 225)

⅓ cup (48 grams) all-purpose flour

Pinch of salt

1 large egg yolk

½ cup (153 grams) raspberry jam

¼ cup (30 grams) confectioners' sugar

1. In the bowl of an electric mixer, using the paddle attachment, combine the butter, sugar, cinnamon, hazelnut flour, all-purpose flour, and salt on low speed. Add the egg yolk and mix just until blended, scraping down the side of the bowl. Remove the dough from the bowl and pat it into a rectangle. Wrap the dough in plastic wrap and refrigerate for at least 2 hours.

2. Line two baking sheets with parchment paper. Unwrap the dough and place it on a lightly floured work surface. Roll it out into a ⅛-inch-thick rectangle. Using a 2½-inch heart-shaped cutter, cut out as many cookies from the dough as you can and place them on the lined baking sheets spacing them 1 inch apart. Pat together the scraps, reroll them, and cut out more cookies. Using a 1-inch heart-shaped cutter, cut out and discard (or bake as extra cookies) the centers from half of the cookies. Refrigerate the cookies for 2 hours.

3. Preheat the oven to 350°F.

4. Bake the cookies for 8 to 10 minutes, or until light golden brown around the edges. Cool the cookies on the baking sheets for 10 minutes. Transfer to a wire rack and cool.

5. Spread the raspberry jam to within ¼ inch from the edge of each whole cookie. Sift the confectioners' sugar over the cutout cookies. Place the sugared cookies on top of the whole cookies, pressing down lightly to sandwich them together. Store the cookies in an airtight container in a cool place for up to 5 days.

Baked Pears in Phyllo

Chocolate Ginger Sauce

½ cup (100 grams) sugar

⅓ cup (79 grams) peeled and chopped ginger

1¾ cups (406 grams) heavy cream

¼ cup plus 2 tablespoons (35 grams) unsweetened alkalized cocoa powder, sifted

Baked Pears

½ cup (100 grams) sugar

1 tablespoon (15 grams) fresh lemon juice

1 vanilla bean, split

4 Bartlett or Bosc pears, peeled but stems left intact

½ cup (105 grams) Almond Cream (page 29)

2 sheets (12 × 17 inches) phyllo dough, thawed if frozen

3 tablespoons (36 grams) Clarified Butter (page 38)

Garnish

2 tablespoons (30 grams) sour cream

4 scoops Vanilla Ice Cream (page 177)

4 mint sprigs

I think of this as an alternative Valentine's Day dessert, because a pear is the most sensuous shape of all foods and because it is a seductive dessert to eat as well. The phyllo encloses a pear stuffed with almond cream; as it bakes, the almond cream puffs up and develops a cakelike texture. You can bake these up to three hours ahead most of the way, then, just prior to serving, bake for another ten minutes or so, until the pears are heated through and the phyllo is crisp. These are served with a ginger-infused chocolate caramel sauce and scoops of vanilla ice cream.

MAKES 4 SERVINGS

Special Equipment:
Pastry Bag Fitted with a ⅜-Inch Plain Tip (Such as Ateco #4)

1. *Make the chocolate ginger sauce:* Combine the sugar with 2 tablespoons (29 grams) water and the ginger in a medium saucepan. Bring to a boil over medium-high heat, stirring until the sugar is dissolved. Boil without stirring until the mixture just begins to caramelize and turn amber. Immediately stir in the cream (be careful, as it may sputter). Reduce the heat to medium and bring the mixture back to a simmer, stirring constantly with a wooden spoon until any hardened bits of caramel are dissolved.

2. Remove the pan from the heat and whisk in the cocoa powder. Strain the sauce through a fine-mesh sieve into a bowl and let cool.

3. *Make the baked pears:* In a saucepan large enough to hold the pears, combine 6 cups (1,416 grams) water with the sugar, and lemon juice. Scrape the seeds from the vanilla bean into the pan and add the bean. Cook over medium-high heat, stirring to dissolve the sugar. Wash down the sides of the pan with a wet pastry brush. Add the pears and bring to a boil. Reduce the heat and simmer over low heat for 18 to 20 minutes, until a fork inserted in the pears enters easily; the pears should still be slightly firm. Allow the pears to cool completely in the syrup.

continued

4. Preheat the oven to 325°F.

5. Remove the pears from the syrup and drain on paper towels. Using an apple or pear corer, core the pears from the bottom, keeping the stems intact. Scrape the almond cream into a pastry bag fitted with a ⅜-inch plain tip. Pipe the cream into the hollows in the pears, filling them completely.

6. Stack the phyllo sheets on a cutting board. Cut the sheets into 1 × 17-inch strips. Place a sheet of plastic wrap over the phyllo to prevent it from drying out while you are wrapping the pears. Remove 2 of the stacked phyllo strips. Starting at the bottom of one of the pears, wrap one of the strips around the pear, overlapping it and spiraling up toward the stem. Continue with a second strip, until the pear is covered. (Don't worry if the pear doesn't look perfect after the first two strips—it will look much better after it is completely wrapped.) Brush the phyllo with clarified butter and repeat the layering and buttering, using 4 more strips. Repeat with the remaining pears (you will have extra phyllo strips).

7. Place the wrapped pears on an ungreased baking sheet and bake for 60 to 65 minutes, until the phyllo is golden brown and crisp.

8. *Serve the pears:* Spoon a small pool of chocolate sauce onto each of four dessert plates. Place a baked pear in the center of each plate. Fill a small parchment cone (see page 17) with the sour cream. Pipe the sour cream over the chocolate sauce around the pears. Place a scoop of vanilla ice cream alongside each pear and garnish with a mint sprig.

Baked Pears in Phyllo

Pets de Nonne

Pets de Nonne

1⅓ cups (193 grams) all-purpose flour

1 teaspoon (5 grams) baking powder

¼ teaspoon (2 grams) salt

3 tablespoons (45 grams) whole milk

3 large eggs

5 tablespoons (71 grams) unsalted butter, softened

2 tablespoons (28 grams) lemon-flavored or light rum

2 tablespoons (30 grams) orange flower water

4 cups (858 grams) vegetable oil, for deep-frying

Confectioners' sugar for dusting

*P*ets de nonne are puffy fritters that are flavored with orange flower water. They are traditionally made at the time of Carnival, or Mardi Gras, in February. They are best served piping hot, and they can also be slit open and filled with jam or with pastry cream lightened with whipped cream (one part whipped cream to three parts pastry cream). Whether served warm or at room temperature, they would be a great addition to your Christmas buffet.

**MAKES ABOUT
30 PETS DE NONNE**

Special Equipment:
Deep-Frying Thermometer

1. In the bowl of an electric mixer fitted with the paddle attachment, combine the flour, baking powder, and salt and blend on low speed. Add the milk and 3 tablespoons (44 grams) water and mix until a crumbly dough forms. Beat in the eggs one at a time, mixing well after each addition. Scrape down the side of the bowl with a rubber spatula and beat at medium speed for 2 minutes, or until the dough is smooth. Beat in the butter 1 tablespoon at a time, until well blended. Add the rum and orange flower water and mix until blended. Scrape down the side of the bowl and beat for another 30 seconds.

2. In a large deep saucepan or deep fryer, heat the oil to 350°F. Line a large baking sheet with two layers of paper towels.

3. Carefully drop the batter by tablespoons into the oil, 4 or 5 at a time. Fry the pets de nonne for about 1 minute, or until light golden brown, turning them once halfway through frying with a slotted spoon. Using the slotted spoon, transfer the fried dough to the paper towel-lined baking sheet. Sprinkle with sifted confectioners' sugar and serve warm.

*Holiday Cakes,
Cookies,
and Bites*

Bugnes

Bugnes are similar to Pets de Nonne (page 213); they are made from a brioche-like dough that is fried, and can be slit open and filled with jam. The difference is that these are formed into graceful swan shapes, and there is no orange flower water. This was a much fussed-over recipe in my father's shop, because there is a rivalry among various provinces in France over which version of bugne is the best. Bugne de Lyon is perhaps the most famous, and this is similar; it is on the crispy side and has the brioche texture. Like pets de nonne, these are traditionally served at Carnival time, and they are best enjoyed warm.

MAKES 12 BUGNES

Special Equipment:
Deep-Frying Thermometer

¼ ounce (1 teaspoon) (8 grams) crumbled fresh yeast

¼ cup (50 grams) sugar

2½ cups (362 grams) all-purpose flour

¼ cup (30 grams) powdered milk

¾ teaspoon (5 grams) salt

2 large eggs

5 tablespoons (71 grams) unsalted butter, softened

Juice of 1 lemon

2 tablespoons (28 grams) dark rum, such as Myers's

4 cups (858 grams) vegetable oil, for deep-frying

Confectioners' sugar for dusting

1. Combine 2 tablespoons (30 grams) warm water with the yeast and a pinch of the sugar in a small bowl and let stand for 10 minutes, or until the yeast bubbles (if it doesn't, it is a sign that the yeast is not active and you should begin with fresh yeast).

2. In the bowl of an electric mixer fitted with the paddle attachment, combine the flour, powdered milk, the remaining sugar, and the salt and blend on low speed. Add the yeast mixture, then add the eggs one at a time, mixing well after each addition. Add the butter one tablespoon at a time, mixing until blended and scraping down the side of the bowl as necessary. Replace the paddle attachment with the dough hook. Add the lemon juice and rum and mix on medium speed for 15 minutes, or until the dough is smooth and shiny and comes away from the side of the bowl. Remove the bowl from the mixer stand, cover the dough with a damp towel, and let rise in a warm place for 1 hour, until doubled.

3. In a large deep saucepan or deep-fryer, heat the oil to 380°F. Line a large baking sheet with two layers of paper towels.

4. While the oil heats, punch the dough down and place it on a lightly floured work surface. Using a rolling pin, roll the dough out to a ¼-inch thickness. Cut the dough into twelve 5 × 2-inch diamonds. Cut a 2½-inch lengthwise slit in the center of each diamond. Slip one of the elongated points through the slit in each and pull it back so that it is pointing in its original direction; it will resemble a swan shape. Fry the bugnes, 3 or 4 at a time, until golden brown, about 1 minute. Remove the bugnes with a skimmer or slotted spoon and drain on the paper towel-lined baking sheet. Sprinkle with sifted confectioners' sugar and serve warm.

Holiday Cakes, Cookies, and Bites

Deep Chocolate Holiday Cake

Deep Chocolate Cake

17 ounces (482 grams) semisweet chocolate, chopped

¾ pound plus 1 tablespoon (3 sticks plus 1 tablespoon) (354 grams)
unsalted butter, cut into tablespoons

4 large eggs, at room temperature

1¼ cups (250 grams) sugar

1 cup (145 grams) all-purpose flour

Garnish

Chocolate Glaze (page 32)

1¾ cups (150 grams) sliced unblanched almonds, toasted
(see page 16)

1. *Make the deep chocolate cake:* Preheat the oven to 350°F. Butter a
9 × 2-inch fluted deep tart pan. Dust the pan with flour and tap out the
excess.

2. Fill a large pot one-third full with water and bring to a simmer. Put
the chocolate and butter into a large bowl and place it over the simmering water. Stir the mixture until completely melted and smooth. Remove
the bowl from the pot and set aside to cool for 10 minutes.

3. Whisk the eggs and sugar in a large bowl until combined. Whisk
in the chocolate mixture until blended. Whisk in the flour just until
blended. Scrape the batter into the prepared pan.

4. Bake for 50 to 55 minutes, until a toothpick inserted into the center of the cake comes out with a few moist crumbs clinging to it. Cool the
cake in the pan on a wire rack for 30 minutes.

5. With a spoon, gently press down all around the edge of the cake to
make it level with the center. Carefully unmold the cake onto the wire
rack and cool completely. When the cake is completely cool transfer it to
a plate and refrigerate for at least 2 hours, or up to 24 hours, until well
chilled.

6. *Garnish the cake:* Reheat the glaze, if necessary, until warm. Pour
the warm glaze onto the center of the chilled cake, letting it drip down
the sides. Use a small metal spatula to smooth the glaze over the sides.
Allow the glaze to set for 5 minutes. Press the almonds onto the sides of
the cake. Serve the cake at room temperature or slightly chilled.

*U*nglazed, this cake is a
perfect *goûter,* the French
word for an after-school treat.
Glazed and perhaps decorated
with chocolate curls, it is a great
birthday cake for a devout chocolate lover, and it is appropriate for
Christmas, or even Thanksgiving.
This is the one I make for my
friends for celebrations. The cake
recipe is a simple matter of blending the ingredients together, and
the glaze is also quick and easy.
The result is a rich, over-the-top
chocolate experience. Though it
contains flour, it will remind you
of a flourless cake. Serve with
Vanilla Ice Cream (page 177).

MAKES 10 SERVINGS

Special Equipment:
9 × 2-Inch-High Fluted Deep
Tart Pan

*Holiday Cakes,
Cookies,
and Bites*

Belgian Waffles

When I was a kid, my parents would take us to feasts in Nice and the surrounding areas. And one of the most important traditions associated with these crowded, bustling street festivals were these waffles, which we call *gaufres*. My parents knew that I would ask for one every time, and they always obliged. The waffles were served warm and crispy, sometimes plain, sometimes with vanilla ice cream and fresh raspberries. Today, these make the perfect centerpiece for a festive holiday brunch. The classic recipe calls for both cream and butter in the batter; that makes for quite an amazing texture, but it is just too rich for the way we like to eat today, so I replaced the cream with milk. The sliced almonds give these a nice nutty flavor and crunch. Serve with berries and vanilla ice cream.

MAKES 4 SERVINGS
(8 Waffles)

Special Equipment:
Waffle Iron for 4-Inch-Square
Belgian Waffles

*Holiday Cakes,
Cookies,
and Bites*

Waffles

¾ cup (181 grams) whole milk

3 tablespoons (38 grams) sugar

1¼ teaspoons (4 grams) active dry yeast

⅔ cup plus 2 tablespoons (115 grams) all-purpose flour

½ teaspoon (4 grams) salt

2 large eggs

½ teaspoon (2 grams) pure almond extract

3 tablespoons (42 grams) unsalted butter, melted and cooled

⅓ cup (28 grams) sliced almonds

Garnish

4 scoops Vanilla Ice Cream (page 177)

½ cup (56 grams) mixed berries, such as raspberries, strawberries, and blueberries

1. *Make the waffles:* Combine the milk with 1 tablespoon (13 grams) of the sugar in a small saucepan and heat over low heat until warm, about 110°F, stirring to dissolve the sugar. Pour the milk into a small bowl and sprinkle the yeast over it. Let stand for 10 minutes, or until the yeast bubbles (if it doesn't, it is a sign that the yeast is not active and you should begin again with fresh yeast).

2. Whisk together the flour, salt, and the remaining 2 tablespoons (25 grams) sugar in a medium bowl. In another bowl, whisk the eggs until blended. Whisk in the yeast mixture and almond extract. Make a well in the center of the flour mixture. Pour the liquid ingredients into the well and gradually whisk them into the dry ingredients until blended. Whisk in the melted butter and almonds. Cover the bowl with plastic wrap and let rest for 2 hours.

3. Preheat the waffle iron. If you want to keep the cooked waffles warm until you've made them all, preheat the oven to 200°F.

4. If they are not nonstick, lightly butter or spray the waffle iron grids. Spoon about ½ cup of the batter onto the hot iron. Use a small metal spatula to spread it evenly over the grids. Close the lid and bake until well browned and set, 3 to 8 minutes, depending on your waffle iron. If desired, keep the waffles warm on a rack in the preheated oven while you make the rest. Place 2 waffles on each dessert plate and garnish each with a scoop of vanilla ice cream and berries.

Belgian Waffles

Candies

I combed through all of my recipes for fine chocolates and candies to arrive at the ones in this chapter. I wanted recipes that would offer different flavors and textures and that, most important, would be easy to make. Feulletine Praline features milk chocolate and crispy cereal—a proven favorite of kids and grown-ups everywhere. My Soft Chocolate Caramels are chewy and flavorful, and Macadamia Nut Toffee is crunchy and delicious.

These five candies are perfect for every occasion and mood, and are especially useful as a hostess gift or as an offering on your holiday dessert table. They can be made a week ahead of time and stored in a cool, dry place.

I promise you, none of them is difficult. I urge you to give them a try. Becoming a candymaker is like winning the lottery; you will suddenly have more friends than you ever thought possible.

Feuilletine Praline

3½ ounces (100 grams) milk chocolate, chopped

¾ cup (50 grams) cocoa butter (see Sources, page 225)

1⅔ cups (500 grams) Praline Paste (page 36, or see Sources, page 225)

4 cups (300 grams) feuilletine (see page 8) or Rice Krispies

1. Fill a medium saucepan one-third full with water and bring to a simmer. Place the chocolate and cocoa butter in a medium bowl, place over the simmering water, and stir until completely melted and smooth. Remove the bowl from the pan and set aside.

2. Line a 17½ × 12½-inch baking sheet with parchment paper. In the bowl of an electric mixer fitted with the paddle attachment, beat the praline paste on low speed for 1 minute, or until softened. Add the chocolate mixture and mix on low speed until well combined, about 1 minute. Remove the bowl from the mixer stand and stir in the feuilletine. Scrape the chocolate mixture onto the prepared baking sheet and, using an offset spatula, spread it into an even layer. Place the praline in the refrigerator for 15 minutes, or until set.

3. Spray a knife with nonstick cooking spray. Cut the praline lengthwise into 1-inch-wide strips, spraying the knife again as necessary. Cut each strip on the diagonal to form 1½-inch-long diamond shapes. Store in an airtight container in a cool dry place for up to 2 weeks.

*K*ids love this candy because it's sweet and crunchy. The feuilletine (or Rice Krispies) nicely balances the praline paste, which is plenty sweet. Although this is not difficult to make, you do need cocoa butter for it.

MAKES ABOUT
100 CHOCOLATES

Candies

Soft Chocolate Caramels

This simple recipe produces caramels that are the opposite of those super-chewy, super-sweet cellophane-wrapped squares you buy in the store. These are soft almost to the point of creamy. Use a chocolate with high cocoa butter content, such as Callebaut, or a couverture chocolate if you can obtain it. Don't worry if you see the fat separate during melting. Just gently stir to remix.

For the caramels I sell in my shop, I use fleur de sel, a hand-harvested salt from Brittany with a subtle, floral aroma. It is excellent, and you don't have to use very much; it is available by mail order (see page 225). If you overcook caramel, it will be bitter; a pinch or two of salt will bring the flavor back. You can make caramels in the traditional squares, or you can create little twists or other fanciful shapes for the kids. You can also dip them in chocolate to make a wonderful bonbon.

MAKES ABOUT 176 CARAMELS

Special Equipment:
Candy Thermometer

12 ounces (340 grams) bittersweet chocolate, finely chopped
2 cups (400 grams) sugar
2 cups (464 grams) heavy cream
1½ cups (492 grams) corn syrup
Pinch of salt, preferably fleur de sel (see page 8)

1. Line a 9 × 13-inch baking pan with parchment paper. Place the chopped chocolate in a large bowl and set aside.

2. Combine the sugar, cream, corn syrup, and salt in a medium saucepan. Bring to a boil over medium-high heat, stirring until the sugar is dissolved. Cook without stirring until the mixture reaches 243°F on a candy thermometer. Immediately pour the mixture over the chocolate and whisk until smooth.

3. Pour the chocolate mixture into the prepared baking pan. Using a small offset metal spatula, spread the mixture into an even layer. Cool for 20 minutes, or until the caramel is cool enough to handle.

4. Line two baking sheets with parchment paper. Spray a knife with nonstick cooking spray. Cut the caramels into ¾-inch squares. Transfer them to the baking sheets and allow to set completely, about 6 hours, or overnight. Store the caramels in an airtight container for up to 1 week.

Candies

Muscadines

Muscadines

17 ounces (482 grams) bittersweet chocolate, finely chopped

¼ cup (75 grams) trimoline (see Note)

2 cups (464 grams) heavy cream

1 teaspoon (1 gram) instant espresso powder

¼ cup (61 grams) Grand Marnier orange liqueur

Coating

9 ounces (255 grams) bittersweet chocolate, chopped

1⅓ cups (153 grams) confectioners' sugar

1. *Make the muscadines:* Place the finely chopped chocolate and the trimoline in a large bowl and set aside.

2. In a medium saucepan, bring the cream to a boil. Remove the pan from the heat and stir in the espresso powder. Immediately pour the hot cream over the chopped chocolate and let stand for 30 seconds. Whisk until smooth. Whisk in the Grand Marnier. Allow the mixture to cool to room temperature, then refrigerate, stirring occasionally, until it is the consistency of pudding. This should take about 45 minutes.

3. Fill a pastry bag fitted with a ½-inch plain tip with the chocolate mixture. Pipe out long logs (about ½-inch wide) of the chocolate on the lined baking sheets. Place the logs in the refrigerator to chill for 15 minutes.

4. *Coat the candies:* Fill a medium saucepan one-third of the way with water and bring to a simmer. Place the chocolate in a medium bowl and place it over the simmering water. Stir until the chocolate is completely melted.

5. Place the confectioners' sugar in a dish or pie pan. Using a sharp knife, cut the chocolate into 1-inch-long logs. Spoon some of the melted chocolate onto your palm. Place a muscadine log on your chocolate covered palm and, using your other hand, roll it around to coat it in the chocolate. Allow the chocolate to set for 5 minutes. Using a fork, roll the coated logs in the confectioners' sugar. Store the muscadines in an airtight container in the refrigerator for up to 2 weeks.

NOTE: Trimoline is what is called an invert sugar. Created by heating a small amount of granulated sugar with an acid, which breaks down (inverts) the sucrose into glucose and fructose, invert sugar has smaller crystals than granulated. It is used in candy making and other desserts to make a smoother consistency.

Orange and coffee are the traditional flavors underlining the chocolate in this delicious candy, which is a classic in France, and has a very festive, wintery holiday look. A whisper-thin chocolate coating encloses the ganache. I call for trimoline, but you can substitute ¼ cup of light corn syrup. You can pipe these in individual tubes, but I recommend that you pipe one long row and cut it into 1¼-inch lengths. These ganache tubes are fragile, even after being chilled, so I recommend that you only chocolate-coat and sugar-roll two at a time. These candies will keep in the refrigerator in an airtight container for two weeks, but when it comes time to serve them, reroll them in confectioners' sugar to refresh them.

**MAKES ABOUT
50 CHOCOLATES**

Special Equipment:
Pastry Bag Fitted with a ½-Inch
Plain Tip (Such as Ateco #6)

Candies

Armagnac Truffles

This recipe is great because the flavor of the ganache can be changed in so many ways that you're certain to find a favorite. Instead of Armagnac (brandy), you can use rum (Myers's or Malibu), Grand Marnier (orange-flavored liqueur), cognac or Calvados (a dry apple brandy). If you use Armagnac, you can add some very finely chopped prune pieces to the ganache. If you use Grand Marnier, you might add very finely chopped orange pieces. One further option for making the perfect truffle: roll the ganache in the melted chocolate, let it set, then coat it again for a very slight double crust.

**MAKES ABOUT
100 TRUFFLES**

Special Equipment:
Pastry Bag Fitted with a ¼-Inch Plain Tip (Such as Ateco #2)

Truffles

17 ounces (482 grams) bittersweet chocolate, finely chopped

2½ tablespoons (50 grams) light corn syrup

2 cups (464 grams) heavy cream

3½ tablespoons (50 grams) Armagnac or cognac

Coating

9 ounces (255 grams) bittersweet chocolate, chopped

1⅔ cups (157 grams) unsweetened alkalized cocoa powder

1. *Make the truffles:* Place the chopped chocolate and corn syrup in a large bowl and set aside.

2. In a medium saucepan, bring the heavy cream to a boil. Pour the hot cream over the chocolate and let stand for 30 seconds. Whisk until smooth. Whisk in the Armagnac. Let cool to room temperature, stirring occasionally, about 15 minutes.

3. Place the chocolate mixture in the refrigerator, stirring occasionally, until it is the consistency of pudding, about 20 minutes.

4. Have a baking sheet lined with parchment paper ready. Fill a pastry bag fitted with a ¼-inch plain tip with the chilled chocolate mixture. Pipe out ¾-inch mounds of the mixture onto the baking sheet. Chill the mounds for 15 minutes.

5. *Coat the truffles:* Fill a medium saucepan one-third of the way with water and bring to a simmer. Place the chocolate in a medium bowl and place it over the simmering water. Stir until the chocolate is completely melted.

6. Place the cocoa powder in a shallow dish or pie pan. Using your palms, roll the chocolate mounds into balls. Dip the truffles, one at a time, into the melted chocolate. Remove the truffles with a fork, allowing the excess chocolate to drip off. Using a fork, immediately roll the truffles in the cocoa powder, coating them completely. Store the truffles in an airtight container in a cool, dry place for up to 2 weeks.

Armagnac Truffles

Macadamia Nut Toffee

This recipe came from Johnny Izzuni, my assistant at Restaurant Daniel. He knew that I like my candies with crunch, and that I'm wild about caramel. For toffee, you cook the caramel a little longer than you do for Soft Chocolate Caramels (page 220); this longer cooking time not only hardens the caramel to a toffee, but it also gives it some flavor bite. An easy way to crush the macadamias is to put them in a towel and hammer them with a rolling pin; they are soft and will break up quickly. You can also dip these in melted chocolate if you like.

MAKES ABOUT 1½ POUNDS

Special Equipment:
Candy Thermometer

1¼ cups (290 grams) heavy cream

2 tablespoons (41 grams) light corn syrup

1⅔ cups (334 grams) sugar

2¾ cups (400 grams) macadamia nuts, crushed

1. Combine the heavy cream, corn syrup, and sugar in a medium heavy saucepan. Bring to a boil over medium-high heat, stirring to dissolve the sugar. Insert a candy thermometer in the pan and boil without stirring until the mixture reaches 284°F. Remove the pan from the heat and stir in the macadamia nuts. Immediately pour the toffee onto the prepared baking sheet. Let cool completely, about 1 hour.

2. Break the toffee into irregular pieces. Store in an airtight container in a cool dry place for up to 2 weeks.

Albert Uster
9211 Gaither Road
Gaithersburg, MD 20877
(800) 231–8154
*Swiss chocolate; baking and confectionery
products, including candied fruits, zests,
and chestnuts; baking equipment, sweetened chestnut purée and candied chestnuts*

Assouline & Ting
314 Brown Street
Philadelphia, PA 19123
(215) 627–3000; (800) 521–4491
*chocolate, fruit purées, extracts, nut
pastes, nut flours*

The Baker's Catalogue
King Arthur Flour
P.O. Box 876
Norwich, VT 05055–0876
(800) 827–6836
*baking equipment and ingredients,
including specialty flours, nut pastes,
vanilla beans, and fleur de sel*

Bridge Kitchenware Corp.
214 East 52nd Street
New York, NY 10022
(212) 838–6746; (800) 274–3435
baking and pastry equipment

DeChoix Specialty Foods
58-25 52nd Avenue
Woodside, NY 11377
(718) 507–8080; (800) 834–6881
*chocolate, fruit purées and pastes, nuts,
nut pastes, nut flours*

Gourmail
126A Pleasant Valley, #401
Methuen, MA 01844
(800) 366–5900, ext. 96
chocolate

J. B. Prince Company
36 East 31st Street
11th Floor
New York, NY 10016
(212) 683–3553
*baking and pastry tools and equipment,
including ring molds, cake rings, tart
and tartlet pans, bûche de noël molds,
charlotte molds*

Kerekes
7107 13th Avenue
Brooklyn, NY 11228
(718) 232–7044; (800) 525–5556
molds, baking tools and equipment

KitchenAid
701 Main Street
St. Joseph, MI 49085–1392
(800) 541–6390
food processors

New York Cake and
Baking Distributors
56 West 22nd Street
New York, NY 10010
(212) 675–CAKE; (800) 94–CAKE-9
*pastry brushes, cake decorating
supplies*

Paris Gourmet Patisfrance
161 East Union Avenue
E. Rutherford, NJ 07073
(800) PASTRY-1
feuilletine (brand name, Crousticrep),
chocolates, nut products, flavoring pastes,
fruit purées, extracts and essences

Penzeys, Ltd.
P.O. Box 933
Muskego, WI 53150
(414) 679-7207
Ceylon cinnamon and other spices, herbs
and seasonings

Previn Inc.
2044 Rittenhouse Square
Philadelphia, PA 19103
(215) 985-1996
digital instant-read thermometer, candy-
making supplies

Sweet Celebrations
(formerly Maid of Scandinavia)
7009 Washington Avenue South
Edina, MN 55439
(800) 328-6722
chocolate, cocoa butter, cake decorating
supplies, chocolate and candy-making sup-
plies, baking and pastry supplies and
equipment

Tropical Nut & Fruit
P.O. Box 7507
1100 Continental Boulevard
Charlotte, NC 28273
(704) 588-0400; (800) 438-4470
chocolate, dried fruits and nuts

White Toque, Inc.
536 Fayette Street
Perth Amboy, NJ 08861
(800) 237-6936
fruit purées

Williams-Sonoma
P.O. Box 7456
San Francisco, CA 94120-7456
(800) 541-2233
chocolate, specialty flours, baking pans
and equipment

Index

Index

Index

Index

Index

PATISSERIE "AU NID D

*"My mother was born here, in my grandfather's pâtisserie.
How could I not have been raised with a love of baking?"*